Praise for *Insights from*
Reading the Bible with the Poor

"This highly important book moves beyond addressing the Bible's potential for transformative social justice; it offers a tested roadmap. Through detailing how marginalized peoples and biblical scholars are effectively working together to confront injustice in their communities, Hall takes engaged biblical scholarship to where it needs to be—the streets."

—Matthew J. M. Coomber, St. Ambrose University

"This is no armchair academic speculation. Crystal L. Hall draws from her lived experience of being embedded with the poor in their struggle against the devastating and demeaning impact of local capitalist enterprises. She has learned firsthand how to listen to the voices of the poor in order to know how to facilitate the reading of biblical texts to evoke insights into particular people's struggles for justice and to insist on their rights and humanity. Scholars and teachers have much to learn from her direct engagement and informed insightful critical reflection. This is liberative praxis."

—Richard A. Horsley, author of *Jesus and Empire* and *Covenant Economics*

"This sparkling text helps us reflect on and challenge unjust structures of our society. A refreshing way of doing theology and academic work. I read Hall's work and got energy and new insights on how important is to do intentional hermeneutics toward transformation."

—Paulo Ueti, Latin American Bible scholar

"Perfect for congregations, classrooms, and community settings, *Insights* will guide and inspire. Hall provides a plainspoken orientation to critical frameworks that shape our understanding of who can interpret the Bible and how. Her vivid narration of history, setting, and facilitation choices for 'reading with' is democratizing pedagogy at its best."

—Noelle Damico, senior fellow, National Economic and Social Rights Initiative

Insights from Reading the Bible with the Poor

Insights from Reading the Bible with the Poor

CRYSTAL L. HALL

FORTRESS PRESS
MINNEAPOLIS

INSIGHTS FROM READING THE BIBLE WITH THE POOR

Print ISBN: 978-1-5064-0278-9
eBook ISBN: 978-1-5064-0279-6

Cover image: Brooklyn Bridge/ Andres Garcia Martin/ Thinkstock & Cruz de Tejeda/
emregologlu/ Thinkstock
Cover design: Rob Dewey

*To the unsung saints of the struggle
—past, present, and future*

Contents

Series Foreword

"What does this mean?"

That is, perhaps, the most-asked question with regard to the Bible. What does this verse mean? What does this story mean? What does this psalm or letter or prophecy or promise or commandment mean?

The question can arise from a simple desire for information, or the concern may be one of context or relevance: What *did* this mean to its original audience? What *does* it mean for us today?

Someone has said that understanding the Bible is difficult not because meaning is hard to find but because it is so abundant. The problem for interpreters is not *too little meaning* but *too much*. The question becomes, Which of all the possible meanings is to be preferred?

But is that really a problem? And, if so, is it not a lovely one?

This abundance of meaning became especially clear in the last decades of the twentieth century when the field of biblical studies embraced dozens of new methods and approaches that had not previously been used or appreciated within the guild. In many ways, biblical studies became more exciting than ever before.

But yes, the task of understanding the Bible could be daunting. Bible teachers, clergy and lay, who had struggled through college or seminary to learn "the historical-critical method" were suddenly confronted with novel strategies drawn from many other fields of inquiry: sociology, psychology, world religions, cultural anthropology, communication theory, modern literary criticism, and so forth. Then came the avalanche of interpretive approaches grounded in particular philosophical or ideological perspectives: feminism, postmodernism, liberation theology, postcolonialism, queer theology, and on and on.

For the open-minded, the yield was an embarrassment of riches. We now understand the Bible in so many different ways: its historical witness, its theological message, its emotional impact, its sociocultural significance, its literary artistry, its capacity for rhetorical engagement, and so on.

At this point in time, we probably understand the Bible better than any who have gone before us. The Bible may challenge us more deeply than it challenged our forebears—and yet we have discovered that the Bible also seems to invite us (perhaps to *dare* us) to challenge it back. Many insights into the meaning of Scripture have come from people doing exactly that.

This Insights series from Fortress Press presents brief volumes that describe different ways in which modern scholars approach the Bible, with emphasis on what we have learned from each of these approaches. These are not boring books on esoteric methodology. Some attention, of course, needs to be paid to presumptions and procedures, but the emphasis in each book is on the practical "pay-off" that a given approach has for students and teachers of the Bible. The authors discuss the most important insights they have gained from their approaches, and they provide examples of how those insights play out when working with specific biblical texts in actual real-world circumstances.

Each volume discusses:

- how a particular method, approach, or strategy was first developed and how its application has changed over time;
- what current questions arise from its use;
- what enduring insights it has produced; and
- what questions remain for future scholarship.

Some volumes feature traditional approaches while others focus on new and experimental ones. You will definitely learn things in every book. Your current understanding of "what the Bible means" will be increased. And if you find that the "type of meaning" gained from a particular approach is not what interests you, perhaps you will nevertheless be grateful for the brief tour of a topic that fascinates some of your peers. The books are intentionally brief: they allow us to sample strategies and perspectives, to look down various avenues and see where they lead. They facilitate informed decisions regarding where we might want to go next.

I trust that we are now past the point of arguing over which approach to Scripture is the correct one. Such squabbles were part of the growth pains associated with the guild's aforementioned discovery that meaning is abundant, not so much elusive as ubiquitous.

Those of us who were professors during the late twentieth century sometimes helped our students deal with the methodological confusion by reminding them of the old Indian fable about six blind men and an elephant. In one well-known version of that tale, each of the blind men encounters an elephant and decides "what an elephant is like" based on his singular experience: one feels the trunk and says an elephant is like a hose; another, the tusk and says it is like a spear; another, the ear and says it is like a fan; another, the side and says it is like a wall; another, the leg and says it is like a tree; another, the tail and says it is like a rope. Later, when the men compare notes, each of them insists that he alone understands what an elephant is like: his comrades are totally mistaken.

So, we told our students in the 1990s, each biblical approach or method yields some valid insight into "the meaning of the Bible" (or into "the mystery of divine revelation" or into "what God wants to say to us"). But we would be wise to listen to those whose experience with the Bible is different from ours.

The Insights series is born of humility: its very existence is testimony to our commitment that we need to compare notes about the Bible with openness to each other's diverse perspectives. But beyond that, I would hope that these volumes might also lead us to admit the limits of our perception. We now see, as the apostle Paul puts it, "in a mirror dimly" (1 Cor 13:12).

Many, including myself, who study the Bible believe it is the word of God, meaning it is a source of divine revelation. For this reason alone, the meaning of the Bible is abundant and ubiquitous. We probably understand the Bible here and now better than any other people in history, and this triumph has brought us to the realization of how little we can understand, now or ever. But, insights? Yes. Those we can claim. Our experiences, our knowledge, and our perspectives do have authenticity, and from them we have at least gained some *insights* into the meaning of Scripture. Time to compare notes!

Mark Allan Powell

Foreword

I write this foreword with joy and in solidarity. My joy derives from witnessing another generation of socially engaged biblical scholars take up the work of rereading the Bible *with* the poor in the quest for systemic justice and change.

Those of us who heeded the call of liberation theologies in the 1970s and 1980s were fortunate to be drawn into and disciplined by various liberation movements around the world. I remember well the formative experience as I, a young white South African, was reschooled by anti-apartheid social movements, which summoned me to use my biblical studies training within a black (race and/or class) project of liberation. The liberation struggles of various postcolonies during the 1970s and 1980s generated organic social movements across kindred struggles. I remember well weeklong workshops with activists from Brazil, the Philippines, and South Africa, working together to forge ways of doing community-based Bible study within the reality of the low-intensity–conflict model being used by each of our governments to control opposition forces. The social movements of the 1970s and 1980s (and even the early 1990s) were formidable cross-contextual spaces of summons, solidarity, struggle, and formation.

I have worried where another generation of activist biblical scholars might find a place within the more fragmented social movements of our contemporary times. So when I first met Crystal L. Hall in 2012 at Union Theological Seminary, New York, I was delighted to engage with a young, socially engaged biblical scholar who was already embedded within an array of organized struggles, including worker-based struggles. Her work with United Workers in Baltimore, for example, demonstrated that she was a young activist who had submitted herself to the organised discipline "from below" a social movement. The formative context of the United Workers movement is evident on almost every page of this book. The realities of working people's struggles have shaped the Bible studies and the facilitation processes that Crystal L. Hall shares with us. So there is a profound sense of joy as I write that I can bear witness to another generation of activist biblical scholars finding a place within the social movements of our contemporary time.

I write this foreword in solidarity. So much of what Crystal L. Hall reflects on in this book resonates with my work over the past thirty years. I stand in solidarity with her as she confronts white supremacy as an ideology of oppression. In the language of comrades in Latin America, white supremacy is an idol of death. I stand in solidarity with her as she intersects systems of oppression, including racism, patriarchy, and capitalism. Her recognition and analysis of poverty as structural is exemplary, grounding her work in this book in intersecting social systems. That economics and class are so fundamental to her contextual analysis, her social location, and her biblical interpretation is remarkable. I remember well the cautionary words of the late Brazilian theologian Milton Schwantes reminding us that the only marginalized sector not invited to the "progressive" conversation table were the poor. The poor are present, indeed formative, in Crystal L. Hall's "reading with" processes.

Networks of solidarity are vital to the work of contextual Bible rereading. Crystal L. Hall honours us by engaging with the work of the Ujamaa Centre here in South Africa so carefully. We have valued our working relationship with her over these many years. Her book now offers us ways of building further solidarity. The book is a valuable resource for our reflections and work. There is much here that we will draw on as we continue our work. For example, the Ujamaa Centre is currently doing extensive work on the intersection of economics, land, and gender. We have returned to the story of the expropriation of Naboth's family land (as told in 1 Kings 21), working with organized groups of unemployed black youth in our region of KwaZulu-Natal. So I have read with care how various sectors, including elderly members of St. Athanasius parish, high school students of Free Your Voice, United Workers members from across Baltimore, city residents, and a handful of representatives from faith-rooted environmental justice groups, have worked with this biblical text. Their voices resonate with our voices as we struggle for justice in our different contexts.

Finally, in this foreword I recognize and affirm how faith is found and forged "in the struggle." The epilogue of Crystal L. Hall's book is a confession of faith. Let us wade in this water indeed.

Gerald O. West

Introduction

The Bible study has been underway for a while. People are gathered in the back of a church under the overhang of the balcony. In the cavernous room all but a few of the stained-glass windows are boarded up. The light comes instead from strung paper lanterns and white Christmas tree lights. Paint is peeling from the ceiling, and the plaster on the walls is cracked. The chancel has been replaced by a stage, and the pulpit repurposed for a mixing board. Where there were once pews is now an open floor, and racks of folding chairs and tables are clustered along the walls. What used to be the grand sanctuary of a Methodist church is now repurposed. The participants sit in a circle on hand-me-down couches spruced up with covers, an ottoman, a rocking chair. Plywood boards painted white, which usually serve as a transportable projector screen, today have become an enormous easel. On this easel is newsprint paper with handwritten questions and responses written in marker.

In the thick of the discussion a man makes what, in the moment, is almost an offhand comment.[1] "We're tired of being the crabs at the bottom of the bucket." Anyone who has visited Baltimore knows the restaurants are famous for crabs. But this man is not alluding to the tourist-fueled crabbing industry but to the folk adage that you never

---

1. This seemingly off-hand comment is an example of when the "hidden transcript" emerges from behind the "public transcript." The "public transcript" is "the open interaction between subordinates and those who dominate" and is "unlikely to tell the whole story about power relations," while the "hidden transcript" is a "discourse that takes place 'offstage,' beyond direct observation by powerholders." James C. Scott, *Domination and the Arts of Resistance: Hidden Transcripts* (New Haven: Yale University Press, 1990), 2, 4. Writing about Contextual Bible Study, West asserts, "The crucial point of Scott's detailed argument is that 'the hidden transcript is a self-disclosure that power relations normally exclude from the official transcript.'" Gerald O. West, *The Academy of the Poor: Towards a Dialogical Reading of the Bible* (Sheffield: Sheffield Academic, 1999), 26. This remark is an example of a "self-disclosure" that begins to tell an "authentic," as opposed to a "masked," story about power relations in our contemporary context.

need to put a lid on a bucket of crabs. Any time a crab tries to climb out, the others pull it back down. Despite their best efforts, all the crabs stay stuck in the bucket. More than that, they will soon be cooked and eaten. The text under discussion was 1 Corinthians 1:18–31, and this illustration of the text's logic has just as much, if not more, resonance with the group as any abstract, scholarly approach to reconstructing it.

A starting point for this book is the people's theologies that emerge "from below" in dialogue with the Bible—from the back of what used to be church sanctuaries, from basements, from sidewalks. These ways of reading the Bible emerge as communities of the organized poor develop theological resources to grapple with the immense and unnecessary suffering they have experienced in their own lives, as well as through coming to an understanding of the political and economic structures that produce it.[2] These people's theologies are grounded in the realities that people must struggle like crabs at the bottom of a bucket. The majority of human life is, unlike the expensive crabs in Baltimore, made cheap. Today's world is one in which people are just as disposable a commodity as the butcher paper that lines the picnic tables at crab shacks. They are not regarded as people, but things.

Another starting point for this book is that in the midst of those most directly affected by poverty are people organizing for social change. Organizing is about building relationships, developing collective understandings about what needs transformation to realize the world we want to live in. Organizing is a gradual recognition of the ways in which we are divided from one another on the basis of our races, genders, and classes. Organizing builds unity across those lines of division by reclaiming an inherent sense of worth and dignity for all involved.[3] In the words of Leonardo Boff,

> The poor are generally regarded as those who do not have food, shelter, clothes, work, culture. Those who have, so it is said, must help those who do not, so as to free them from the inhumanity of poverty. This strategy is full of good will and is well meaning; it is the basis for all assistance and paternalism in history. However, it is neither efficient nor sufficient. It does

2. It is my position that poverty is the result of a political and economic structure that is inherently poverty producing. In contradistinction to many "common-sense" understandings, poverty today is not a pathology resulting from the attitudes, behaviors, or values of people in poverty. It is not an accident as a result of the boom-and-bust cycles of the economy, or being in the wrong place at the wrong time. For an in-depth analysis of these theories of impoverishment, see William W. Goldsmith and Edward J. Blakely, *Separate Societies: Poverty and Inequality in U.S. Cities* (Philadelphia: Temple University Press, 1992). An additional theory of poverty as "fate" or ordained by God will be addressed in chapter 1.

3. Willie Baptist and Jan Rehmann, *Pedagogy of the Poor: Building the Movement to End Poverty* (New York: Teachers College, 2011), 7–8.

not liberate the poor, because it keeps them in a situation of dependence; worse yet, it does not even appreciate the liberating potential of the poor. The poor are not simply those who do not have; they *do* have. They have culture, the ability to work, to work together, to get organized and to struggle. Only when the poor trust their potential, and when the poor opt for others who are poor, are conditions truly created for genuine liberation.[4]

There are organized communities of people articulating—based on their own knowledge, experience, and analysis—a vision and plan for bringing about a world in which poverty can and must be abolished so that basic needs are met, and human rights and the survival of the earth are ensured. These are communities that struggle to reclaim their humanity, which is constantly denied because we live in a world in which they have become nothing more than crabs at the bottom of the bucket. It is to these communities that this book is accountable, and it aims toward tipping over the bucket and envisioning new ways for the crabs to relate to one another.

Poverty and growing inequality, the tremendous wealth concentrating at the very top, and the growing ranks of those at the bottom, are among the defining issues of our time.[5] This book wrestles with the historical and present realities of how the Bible has been used to justify unfathomable levels of human suffering, violence, pain, and hatred. Ironically, the same Bible can be a resource for liberation, a wellspring from which to ground a vision of abundant life for people and the planet. It is out of processes of reading the Bible with the organized poor that theological and spiritual resources are developed, as one type of knowledge among many, used by communities in struggle. This book explores one methodology through which the Bible can be read as a resource for liberation.

This methodology, here named "reading the Bible with the poor," draws on lineages from both the United States and countries across the globe. One tradition is the Contextual Bible Study (CBS) methodology that grew out of the South African struggle against apartheid. Practitioners of this methodology are based at the Ujamaa Centre for Biblical and Theological Community Development and Research. CBS works as "an emerging interface [for] socially engaged biblical scholars and poor and marginalized 'readers' of the Bible . . . [it is] a form of Bible reading that begins with an emancipatory interest that is grounded in

---

4. Leonardo Boff, *Cry of the Earth, Cry of the Poor*, trans. Phillip Berryman (Maryknoll, NY: Orbis, 1997), 108.

5. Baptist and Rehmann, *Pedagogy of the Poor*, 1.

the real conditions of poor and marginalized local communities."[6] CBS is informed by the See-Judge-Act method, which undertakes "analysis of the local context (See), and then re-reads the Bible to allow the biblical text to speak to the context (Judge), and then moves to action as we respond to what God is saying (Act)."[7] While the CBS methodology originated in the KwaZulu-Natal region of South Africa, biblical scholars, organic intellectuals, and communities of the organized poor have taken it across the African continent,[8] in Europe and the United States,[9] and in other places across the globe. CBS is the primary methodology on which the workshops described in chapters 2 and 3 are based, and there are additional streams of tradition that play an important role in reading the Bible with the poor in the US context.

Another tradition on which this book draws is rooted in the base communities and popular movements of Brazil and is called the "Popular Reading of the Bible" methodology. The Centro de Estudos Bíblicos (CEBI) is an organizational home for this method. Founded in 1979, CEBI works at the intersection of biblical scholarship and popular readings. In the words of Carlos A. Dreher, in this tradition

> it's not biblical scholarship that is important. What is important is what people do in relation to their lives. What is important is the transformation of the reality of suffering, sadness, fear, lack of hope. And this will only occur if what we learn from the Bible is concretized, is materialized in practice . . . The ultimate objective is to transform reality, to alter the coordinates of reality that cause oppression, to root up the evil.[10]

---

6. West, *Academy of the Poor*, xi.

7. "Contextual Bible Study (CBS)," Ujamaa Centre for Biblical and Theological Community Development and Research, https://tinyurl.com/yxzrekqx.

8. One example of the influence of the Contextual Bible Study methodology beyond South Africa across the African continent is the Tamar Campaign, which through reading the rape of Tamar in 2 Samuel 13:1–22 has opened discussions at the intersections of gender-based violence, culture, and the church. See Gerald O. West and Phumzile Zondi-Mabizela, "The Bible Story That Became a Campaign: The Tamar Campaign in South Africa (and Beyond)," *Ministerial Formation* 103 (July 2004): 4–12.

9. For the influence of Contextual Bible Study (CBS) in Europe, particularly in Scotland, see John Riches et al., *What Is Contextual Bible Study?: A Practical Guide with Group Studies for Advent and Lent* (London: Society for Promoting Christian Knowledge, 2010). For examples of the influence of CBS in the United States, see Cheryl B. Anderson, "Lessons on Healing from Naam (2 Kings 5:1–27): An African American Perspective," in *African Women, HIV/AIDS, and Faith Communities*, ed. Isabel Apawa Phiri, Beverley Haddad, and Madipoane Masenya, 23–43 (Pietermaritzburg: Cluster, 2003); and Margaret P. Aymer, *Repairers of the Breach: Five Bible Studies on Social Justice in New Orleans in the Wake of Hurricane Katrina* (Presbyterian Church [USA], 2007).

10. Carlos A. Dreher, *The Walk to Emmaus*, trans. Paulo Ueti Barasioli (São Leopoldo: Centro de Estudos Bíblicos, 2004), 56.

This focus on the concrete and material realities of suffering is rooted in liberation theology in the Latin American context. Like the Ujamaa Centre, CEBI also uses the See-Judge-Act method and adds two additional elements: Celebrate and Evaluate.[11] The reading process occurs among the intersections of the "hermeneutical triangle" of reality, the Bible, and community.[12] Similar to other traditions of popular reading in Latin America, CEBI is committed to reading the Bible from the perspectives of everyday people.

A third tradition from which this book draws is the practice of reading in the US American context in communities of organized struggle that draw their ancestry back to the civil and welfare rights movements of the 1960s, the labor movement of the 1930s, and ultimately the abolitionist movement in the nineteenth century.[13] Organizations committed to this work include the Kairos Center for Religions, Rights, and Social Justice (formerly the Poverty Initiative), and the Center and Library for the Bible and Social Justice. These approaches to reading the Bible with the poor draw on the methodologies in biblical scholarship, but what distinguishes them is dialogue not only with the academy but also with the church and communities of the organized poor in the US context.

In each of these traditions, Contextual Bible Study, Popular Reading of the Bible, and Reading the Bible with the Poor, the experience of struggle is the starting point. Struggle is the school from which biblical interpretation emerges.[14]

11. "Contextual Bible Study (CBS)."

12. "The CEBI Method," Centro de Estudos Bíblicos, https://tinyurl.com/yyhxnpy6.

13. For examples of reading the Bible with the poor in the United States, see Liz Theoharis, *Always with Us?: What Jesus Really Said about the Poor* (Grand Rapids: Eerdmans, 2017); Liz Theoharis and Willie Baptist, "Reading the Bible with the Poor: Building a Social Movement Led by the Poor, as a United Social Force," in *Reading the Bible in an Age of Crisis: Political Exegesis for a New Day*, ed. Bruce Worthington (Minneapolis: Fortress, 2015), 21–52; Willie Baptist and Noelle Damico, "Building the New Freedom Church of the Poor," *Cross Currents* 55, no. 3 (Fall 2005): 352–63; Willie Baptist, Noelle Damico, and Liz Theoharis, "Responses of the Poor to Empire, Then and Now," *Union Seminary Quarterly Review* 59, no. 3–4 (2005): 162–71; Noelle Damico and Gerardo Reyes Chavez, "Determining What Is Best: The Campaign for Fair Food and the Nascent Assembly in Philippi," in *The People Beside Paul: The Philippian Assembly and History from Below*, ed. Joseph A. Marchal, 247–84 (Atlanta: Society of Biblical Literature, 2015); Noelle Damico, "The Intellectual and Social Impact of an Engaged Scholar: Richard A. Horsley's Legacy," in *Bridges in New Testament Interpretation: Interdisciplinary Advances*, ed. Neil Elliott and Werner H. Kelber, 255–310 (New York: Lexington, 2018).

14. Richard Pithouse, "Struggle Is a School: The Rise of the Shackdwellers' Movement in Durban, South Africa," *Monthly Review* 57, no. 9 (February 1, 2006), 30–51.

FOR WHOM IS THIS BOOK WRITTEN?

This book is for anyone curious about how to use the Bible as a resource for liberation. It is for faith leaders and community organizers as much as it is for biblical scholars because it draws on experiences at the intersections of academia, the church, and communities of organized struggle. It is written with an eye toward praxis in order that sharing from my own experience might create space for others to reflect on their own, as well as places from which to further develop this method.

While not an obvious choice, I have chosen to focus on poverty in the United States because it is the context in which I have experienced it most directly. It is the context from which the communities in which I have been embedded read. The US is one of the global contexts perhaps least likely to be associated with poverty, despite the international attention it has received from the likes of the United Nations.[15] I have also chosen to focus on the US instead of other countries so as to, in a small way, not replicate the neocolonial and paternalistic tendencies that US Americans, even with the best of intentions, often replicate when working in so-called "third world" contexts. The struggle for healing and liberation needs to start at home.

Likewise, it would also be easy to fetishize and glamorize Baltimore as a city of black poverty that is completely unrelatable and "other." While any city (or rural community) has its particularities that must be honored, I will explore through this volume how each respective context in which the Bible is read is rooted in the same political, social, and economic systems of oppression. There must be a preferential option, wherever they evolve, for communities of organized struggle committed to liberation in its myriad forms. While poverty certainly looks different in the US, and Baltimore in particular, than in other parts of the world, there is significance in this volume about reading from the proverbial "belly of the beast" that is the US.

I write from the perspective of a "trained reader," acknowledging that I am the product of contexts that have shaped my perspective and, in some ways, narrowed my vision. As a product of academia, I have been trained in certain ideological assumptions that it would require a volume in itself to examine and unpack. My perspective has also been shaped as a white woman who grew up middle class with the educational privilege that comes with a PhD in biblical studies. Acknowledging these perspectives, I also have made the choice again and again over the past decade

15. Philip Alston, "Report of the Special Rapporteur on Extreme Poverty and Human Rights on His Mission to the United States of America," May 4, 2018, https://tinyurl.com/y2wrry79.

to be partially constituted by perspectives different from my own and to see my own life experiences from different perspectives. Here is a brief story as an illustration of this point.

The year I was finishing my doctorate, I whacked my head on a metal staircase, not paying attention, while I was checking the mail in my apartment building. I spent the night in the emergency room and was diagnosed with a concussion. A few weeks later the bills started coming for this relatively minor injury. The first seemed reasonable, but then they kept coming: $200 for this, $300 for that. At the time I was working full-time as a community organizer but could not cover graduate school and medical bills on top of my regular expenses. I started renting my apartment through Airbnb on weekends. Then my partner and I got second jobs cleaning Verizon retail stores. My thought while taking out the trash and dusting cellphone display cases was always, *If only my advisor could see me now.* I felt like I was living two, or even three, lives—one as an organizer organizing low-wage workers, one as a low-wage worker myself, and one as a graduate student fronting as middle class.

While I do not claim to live at the margins of society, I could easily be one medical crisis away from bankruptcy (a possibility had my injury been more serious). On a structural level, I have far more in common as a seminary professor with a day laborer than I do with the people who own the corporations that sell both of us the media, food, housing, and healthcare we consume on a daily basis. The levels of inequality in the US have become so vast that the differences between the so-called middle class and the poor are becoming increasingly irrelevant in comparison to the tremendous gap between the rich and the rest of us. I share this story not to claim poverty but to demonstrate the precariousness of the economic system in which we live and the importance of being able to understand that experience from the perspective of organized struggle.

WHAT'S IN THIS BOOK?

This book explores one method for reading the Bible in communities of organized poor through for the sake of liberation. While in practice it can be difficult to separate out "why" to read the Bible with the poor from "how" to go about it, I have attempted to pull these questions slightly apart for the purposes of clarity by first articulating the principles that underpin the methodology, providing two concrete examples, and then finally distilling some of the principles of facilitation in the method.

Chapter 1 outlines a number of ideological considerations for reading the Bible with the poor in the US. It begins with the theoretical basis for ideologies of oppression, and then three categories of oppression in terms of race, gender, and class. Organized struggle is then explored as a response to these ideologies of oppression.

Chapters 2 and 3 provide concrete examples of reading the Bible with the poor. The organization in which each Bible study was embedded was United Workers, a human rights organization based in Baltimore committed to ending poverty through developing and uniting low-wage workers. Each chapter begins and ends with descriptions of the campaigns in which the Bible studies were developed. Chapter 2 explores the story of Naboth's vineyard (1 Kgs 21:1–16) in light of Free Your Voice's campaign to stop the construction of what would have been the nation's largest trash-burning incinerator. In chapter 3 both the tomb at the end of Mark's Gospel (Mark 16:1–8) and the "vacants" in Baltimore are explored as places of emptiness and abandonment as well as sites of (potential) resurrection.

Reflecting on the processes described in the previous two chapters, chapter 4 focuses specifically on facilitation. It first addresses methodological principles of facilitation for reading the Bible with the poor and then addresses concrete practices of facilitation. The chapter concludes by addressing pitfalls and challenges to facilitation that have evolved out of the experiences described in the previous chapters.

While each of these chapters is intended as part of a whole, they can also stand individually. I offer them as a resource for anyone interested in reading the Bible from the perspective of the organized poor.

1.

Ideological Groundings and Methodology

This chapter outlines some of the overall ideological underpinnings and methodological considerations for reading the Bible with the poor in US American contexts. It takes a step back to examine questions of why one might read the Bible through this particular lens. First, this chapter explores the historical roots in antiquity that ground contemporary constructions of the "Self" over and against the "Other," because the poor are typically defined as "Other." Then it focuses on how these constructions have been expressed historically and in contemporary US American society through race, gender, and class. These "ideologies of oppression" are named as white supremacy, patriarchy, and capitalism, and the concrete physical, psychological, and spiritual manifestations of each are explored in brief. This chapter focuses on poverty as a consequence of capitalism in more detail than the other two.

One response to these ideologies of oppression imposed "from above" is to offer alternative forms of ideological formation "from below." These alternatives are embodied in struggles to change systems of oppression into more life-giving modes of being and organization. In this struggle for liberation, although a contested terrain, the Bible has historically been, and can today be, successfully claimed as a resource. Reading the Bible with the poor intentionally and deliberately locates it within communities of the organized poor out of a commitment to struggle. A consequence of reading from this place is an epistemological shift in which new forms of knowledge outside the traditional realm of biblical studies emerge.

1

Aristotelian Binaries

The origins of the Western conception of the relationship between "Self" and "Other," and by extension the "otherness" of people in poverty, are ancient. They are rooted not in the biblical tradition but in Greek thought and have shaped Western civilization for millennia. As early as the sixth and fifth centuries BCE, Greek philosophers argued that the "beginnings" or "components" of the cosmos existed specifically in binary and hierarchical pairs of opposites.[1] The Greeks developed this system to conceptualize both the natural world and human society.[2]

In the fourth century BCE Aristotle defined the organization of what is "superior" and "inferior" specifically in terms of privation, a loss or lack of something. For example, "female," according to this conception, is "lacking" the definitive characteristics of "male." Aristotle writes, "For the female is like a deformed male, and the menses are semen, only not pure."[3] In addition to male and female, other categories with which Aristotle associated this superior/inferior construction included light/darkness and good/evil.[4] By comparing concepts like male and female to good and evil, these ideas can combine not only to describe but to moralize. Therefore, the superior "Self" is associated not only with the "male" and "light" but also with "good." Using these same categories, the inferior "Other" is then associated with "female," "darkness," and "evil."[5] While the roots of this way of organizing the world and one's place in it are ancient, these binaries continue to express themselves in myriad ways today.

In US American society the relationship between "Self" and "Other" is constructed both individually and collectively.[6] Rooted in the ancient ideas described above, a handful of examples in today's context include: mind over body (and relatedly, the spiritual over the material, and theory

---

1. M. R. Wright, *Cosmology in Antiquity* (New York: Routledge, 1995), 75.

2. G. E. R. Lloyd, *Polarity and Analogy: Two Types of Argumentation in Early Greek Thought* (Cambridge: Cambridge University Press, 1966), 31.

3. Aristotle, *Generation of Animals with an English Translations by A.L. Peck* (Cambridge, MA: Harvard University Press, 1953), 737a.

4. Aristotle, *The Metaphysics with an English Translation by Hugh Tredennick* (Cambridge, MA: Harvard University Press, 1956–1958), 1004b.

5. Brigitte Kahl, *Galatians Re-Imagined: Reading with the Eyes of the Vanquished* (Minneapolis: Fortress, 2010), 17. For a historical survey of the development of these hierarchical binaries in both the Greek philosophical and biblical traditions, see Crystal L. Hall, *From Cosmos to New Creation: A Call to Justice with Earth in Galatians* (Lanham, MD: Rowman and Littlefield, forthcoming).

6. These hierarchical binaries express themselves across many cultures, not just the US American context. In this volume I've chosen to limit myself to the particularities of the US American context.

over praxis), human over earth, rational over emotional, male over female, straight over queer, white over color/dark, thin over fat, rich over poor, able over disabled, and documented over undocumented. In combination, in the US American context, the idealized "Self," among other things, is a straight, cisgender, white, highly educated, wealthy man. ("Cisgender" means a person has the same gender identity as the sex that person was assigned at birth. For example, I was assigned to the female sex at birth and continue to identify as a woman.) Anything "less" is, to varying degrees, "Other," as a woman, a person of color, a person who is poor, and so on. As they were in antiquity, these categories are overlaid with systems of meaning and morality. Therefore, the idealized "Self" is superior not only in terms of his race, gender, and class but also is perceived as morally upright and "good." Anything "less" can be treated with suspicion as morally compromised and "evil." This construction of the superior "Self" over and against the inferior "Other" is deeply rooted in the DNA of US American society.

In addition to defining "superior" and "inferior" types of people, these categories construct social and cultural norms. To provide an example from antiquity, "Already Aristotle had supplemented the *male-female* hierarchy by other relationships related to the order (*nomos*) of the household (*oikos*) or city-state (*polis*). These relations included, for example, the rule of masters over slaves and parents over children—but also the overarching superiority of Greeks over barbarians."[7] These hierarchies expressed themselves materially through the organization of Greek civilization. Likewise, they express themselves in contemporary life in a variety of ways. Leonardo Boff describes them this way from his Brazilian context:

> Capital has been separated from labor, work from leisure, person from nature, man from woman, body from spirit, sex from affection, efficiency from poetry, wonder from organization, God from the world. One of these two poles has come to dominate the other, thereby giving rise to anthropocentrism, capitalism, materialism, patriarchy, machismo, secularism, and monarchical un-trinitarian monotheism.[8]

To provide a contemporary example, in the US American academy, theory is typically valued as the highest ideal over and against praxis, which is often treated with disdain. This value is an expression of valuing the mind and the abstract as superior to the body and the

---

7. Kahl, *Galatians Re-Imagined*, 19.

8. Leonardo Boff, *Cry of the Earth, Cry of the Poor*, trans. Phillip Berryman (Maryknoll, NY: Orbis, 1997), 68.

material. Ironically, though, within US American culture more broadly, the opposite ideal exists. Pragmatism, and even anti-intellectualism, is more highly valued than the "life of the mind." What one "does" is more important than what one "thinks." "Thinking" is often seen as an elitist luxury for which the majority do not "have time."[9] While there are any number of complexities that could be unraveled in this comparison, I provide this brief example to illustrate how binaries shape not only identities but cultural norms.

As will be explored below, constructions of the "Self" in relationship to "Others" express themselves both individually and collectively and define "otherness" not only in terms of poverty. While these relationships shape how people think about themselves and the people around them, they also express themselves materially in concrete and specific ways. They construct ideologies of oppression that have physical, psychological, and spiritual consequences.

IDEOLOGIES OF OPPRESSION

Before turning to how ideologies of oppression express themselves materially, I will briefly define "ideology" by way of example. Near the beginning of the sci-fi film *The Matrix*, the character Morpheus explains to the protagonist Neo the nature of the Matrix, the computer-simulated world that enslaves almost all of humanity to intelligent machines. Morpheus tells Neo,

> The Matrix is everywhere. It is all around us, even now in this very room. You can see it when you look out your window, or when you turn on your television. You can feel it when you go to work, when you go to church, when you pay your taxes. It is the wool that has been pulled over your eyes to blind you from the truth.

Neo asks, "What truth?" Morpheus answers, "That you are a slave, Neo. That you were born into bondage, into a prison that you cannot taste or smell or touch, a prison for your mind."[10]

Ideologies of oppression are exactly that, a "prison of the mind." They are modes of thinking into which people are encultured from birth and are mostly considered normative. They can express themselves in everyday activities like going to work, going to church, and paying

9. For the implications of US American pragmatism for social movements, see Willie Baptist and Jan Rehmann, *Pedagogy of the Poor: Building the Movement to End Poverty* (New York: Teachers College, 2011), 3, 141–42.

10. Lana Wachowski and Lilly Wachowski, *The Matrix* (Los Angeles: Warner Bros., 1999).

one's taxes. They are conceptions of "the way the world works," the way "things were intended to be," "what is expected," or even the "created order God ordained."

In the same scene Morpheus continues, "Unfortunately, no one can be told what the Matrix is. You have to see it for yourself." How one "sees" is critical to understanding ideologies of oppression. The word *ideology* is derived "from the Greek sense of *eidos* as visual image." The study of ideology is an investigation of "the *perceptions* upon which . . . [ideas] were founded."[11] Ideology is concerned with how individuals and groups "see"—how they see themselves in relationship to the world, in relationship to each other, and in relationship to "Others," including people who are poor. Regardless of one's individual position within US American society, people are conditioned to "see" in certain ways, to consider certain things as "given" or "normal." At the same time, how individuals and groups "see" is largely determined by categories such as race, gender, and class. If individuals or groups benefit from a certain ideology it can be difficult to "see" how it functions, while for others who do not benefit, they may have no choice but to "see."

Ideologies of oppression are specifically those perceptions, those ways of seeing the world, that define the "Self" over and against "Others," the "worthy" as superior to the "unworthy." These perceptions obscure the fact that some people benefit from these ideologies and others are oppressed by them. Among the most predominant ideologies that condition how people in the US perceive the world are the interlocking systems of white supremacy, patriarchy, and capitalism. These ideologies define—in terms of race, gender, and class—who fully constitutes a "human being," a "Self," and who approximates, to varying degrees, the "non-human" and "Other." They define who counts, who has value, and who does not. These ideologies express themselves politically, economically, socially, culturally, and institutionally. They pervade every aspect of how US American society is organized, from educational systems, to faith communities, to the government.

These ideological systems are invested with tremendous power. To determine who is worthy of the label "human" and who is "non-human" is to wield the power of life and death. These systems have been invested with a power that belongs to God alone. The Greek word *eidos*, from which *ideology* is derived, is also the same root for *idol*. Idolatry attributes God-like qualities, ultimate power, to things that are not God. Idolatry worships things that are not God.

11. Jan Rehmann, *Theories of Ideology: The Powers of Alienation and Subjection* (Boston: Brill, 2013), 15–16 (my emphasis).

When white supremacy treats people of European descent as the ultimate achievement of civilization, that is idolatry. When women are expected to treat their husbands as gods—when cooking, cleaning, and raising children are exclusively defined as inferior "women's work"—that is idolatry. When capitalism is treated as "the way things work" instead of as a product of history, that is idolatry. And when it is said, "Well, that's just the way things are," or "Put up and shut up," that too is idolatry because it assumes inevitability. It lacks historical context, a recognition that there is a beginning and an ending to all things.

I will treat each of these ideologies of oppression individually and then briefly address the ways in which they interact with one another. White supremacy and patriarchy will be treated more briefly with an emphasis on capitalism. In surveying each of these ideologies, I provide a few caveats up front. First, the study of each represents large fields in terms of economics, history, political science, critical race theory, women's studies, gender, and queer studies. The studies of white supremacy, patriarchy, and capitalism each have their own histories and traditions, literatures, theorists, and practitioners. I am by no means attempting to provide a comprehensive survey of any of these topics but instead seek to provide a brief, broad overview as well as a few concrete examples of how these systems express themselves in lived reality.

Second, the primary categories through which I am choosing to interrogate ideologies of oppression are race, gender, and class. However, it is important to acknowledge that there are other significant categories through which certain people are valued more than others—ability, language, age, size, religion, immigration status, and country of origin, among others. Each of these categories has also evolved ideologies of oppression that divide humanity into superior and inferior categories.

Third, while I treat these ideologies separately for the sake of clarity, they are inherently overlapping. I will explore the ways in which they intersect more specifically below but at the outset want to point out that it can be difficult, if not impossible, to separate issues of race, gender, and class in explicitly "pure" or "discrete" categories.

With these caveats in mind I now turn to each ideology of oppression—white supremacy, patriarchy, and capitalism—individually. Each expresses how the fully human "Self" is constructed over and against less-than-human "Others."

White Supremacy

White supremacy is the racist belief that whites are superior to people of all other races, and that because of this superiority, whites should control and dominate all other races.[12] White supremacy typically considers people who are Jewish an inferior race. Race is socially constructed, and therefore not all peoples of European descent have always been considered white. For example, at the turn of the twentieth century the Irish immigrating to the US were considered black.[13] According to white supremacy peoples of European descent are more "advanced" and "civilized" in comparison to black, brown, and indigenous peoples descended from other parts of the world. In subtle and not-so-subtle ways, people of color are pathologized as "primitive" and "barbaric." While whites who benefit from white supremacy may not think of themselves as racist, they nevertheless profit from the "invisible systems conferring unsought racial dominance" on whites.[14] Part of how white supremacy perpetuates itself is that whites cannot or are unwilling to "see" the ways in which they receive privileges and benefit from white supremacy. Their privilege obscures their vision. Broadly, under white supremacy humanity is divided between the superior white "Self" and inferior non-white "Others."

Patriarchy

Patriarchy is an ideology of oppression in which men dominate and control women based on the perceived inferiority of women.[15]

12. For a preliminary set of resources specifically for whites seeking racial justice, see Eduardo Bonilla-Silva, *Racism without Racists: Color-Blind Racism and the Persistence of Racial Inequality in the United States* (Lanham, MD: Rowman and Littlefield, 2003); Robin J. DiAngelo, *White Fragility: Why It's So Hard for White People to Talk about Racism* (Boston: Beacon, 2018); Tema Okun, *The Emperor Has No Clothes: Teaching about Race and Racism to People Who Don't Want to Know* (Charlotte: Information Age, 2010); and Amy Sonnie and James Tracy, *Hillbilly Nationalists, Urban Race Rebels, and Black Power: Community Organizing in Radical Times* (Brooklyn: Melville House, 2011). For a particularly faith-based perspective, see Jennifer Harvey, *Dear White Christians: For Those Still Longing for Racial Reconciliation* (Grand Rapids: Eerdmans, 2014); Robert P. Jones, *The End of White Christian America* (New York: Simon and Schuster, 2016); and Jim Wallis, *Racism, White Privilege, and the Bridge to a New America* (Grand Rapids: Brazos, 2016).

13. Noel Ignatiev, *How the Irish Became White* (New York: Routledge, 1995).

14. Peggy McIntosh, "White Privilege: Unpacking the Invisible Knapsack," 1989, https://tinyurl.com/y7u82cmg.

15. For a preliminary set of resources on biblical interpretation from feminist, womanist, and mujerista perspectives, see Wilda C. Gafney, *Womanist Midrash: A Reintroduction to the Women of the Torah and the Throne* (Louisville: Westminster John Knox, 2017); Ada María Isasi-Díaz, *En*

The superiority of men is inaccurately attributed not only to perceived biological traits like strength but also to psychological traits like rationality in comparison to the perceived physical weakness, as well as the perceived emotionalism—even hysteria—of women. As with white supremacy, in addition to the alleged physical and psychological superiority of men, moral dimensions are layered on in which men are understood as good and women as evil. Like the "curse of Ham" which was used to justify slavery, millennia of patriarchal interpretations of Genesis have condemned women as the source of evil. These interpretations surmise that sin came into the world through Eve's temptation of Adam in Eden. Women's inherently sinful natures must therefore be constrained through men's careful control. Men seek to control women's bodies and their sexual reproduction through the institution of marriage and other means. Like Africans being reduced to property as slaves, women's bodies have been reduced to objects available for admiration, sexual gratification, and bearing children. In sum, patriarchy divides humanity between superior men and inferior women.

While I have focused in the above paragraph on women, it is also important to note that patriarchy functions on a strictly binary definition of gender that marginalizes and "feminizes" other forms of gender expression and sexual identity, namely people of the LGBTQIA+ community.[16] Recent innovations in gender studies have demonstrated that gender does not exist in a strict binary in which men and women are inherently opposite but that gender identity and sexual orientation function on a spectrum in which a person may fall between the "extremes" of stereotypical femininity and masculinity.[17] Heteronormativity, as an expression of patriarchy, assumes people who do not conform to these stereotypical gender norms are deviant. According to this standard, the only "normal" sexual relationships are those between straight men and straight women. Patriarchy is for these reasons an ideology of oppression not only for women but also for people who identify as LGBTQIA+.

la Lucha = In the Struggle: A Hispanic Women's Liberation Theology (Minneapolis: Fortress, 1993); Nyasha Junior, An Introduction to Womanist Biblical Interpretation (Louisville: Westminster John Knox, 2015); Elisabeth Schüssler Fiorenza, In Memory of Her: A Feminist Theological Reconstruction of Christian Origins (New York: Crossroad, 1983); Fernando F. Segovia, "Mujerista Theology: Biblical Interpretation and Political Theology," Feminist Theology 20, no. 1 (September 2011): 21–27; Phyllis Trible, God and the Rhetoric of Sexuality (Philadelphia: Fortress, 1978).

16. While many may be familiar with the more standard LGBT to identify the lesbian, gay, bisexual, and transgender community, I intentionally use the more expansive LGBTQIA+ to also include people who identify as queer or questioning, intersex, and asexual. The "+" includes the myriad other ways in which a person might choose to identify that are not included in the previous letters.

17. Joel Baum, "Gender Spectrum," in The Sage Encyclopedia of LGBTQ Studies, ed. Abbie E. Goldberg, 452–56 (Thousand Oaks, CA: SAGE, 2016).

Having surveyed white supremacy and patriarchy as ideologies of oppression in brief, I will now turn to capitalism.

Capitalism

Before turning to capitalism directly, I will make a few comments about what distinguishes capitalism from white supremacy and patriarchy as an ideology of oppression. While the latter are both pervasive within US society, there is far more social consensus about the harmful structures of both white supremacy and patriarchy. While often caught up in discourses about political correctness in the US American context, it is increasingly unacceptable to express overtly racist beliefs. That the majority of whites do not recognize themselves as beneficiaries of white supremacy demonstrates just how much work is still to be done toward racial reconciliation. Similarly, there is near unanimous agreement that the abuse of women and children is unacceptable and a growing consensus that it is objectionable to discriminate against people who identify as LGBTQIA+. While white supremacy and patriarchy are still normative in many respects in the US, significant strides have been made to protect the civil and political rights of women and people who identify as LGBTQIA+, although these protections can certainly not be taken for granted.

However, there is far less consensus that capitalism is an oppressive ideology; many, if not most, people in the US consider capitalism to be the height of Western civilization, or at the very least (in the words of former British prime minister Margaret Thatcher), there is no alternative. It is true that there is more wealth and productive capacity available to humanity now than there has been at any point in human history. While neoliberal economic values such as competition and individualism dominate US culture, in the wake of the 2008 financial crisis and the Occupy movement, there is perhaps more openness now to alternative economic systems than there has ever been, especially among young people.[18] While it would be a book in itself to detail the beneficial and oppressive aspects of capitalism, it is my position that, on a structural basis, the capitalist system is fundamentally exploitative and therefore oppressive.

Capitalism is the global economic system that currently defines who

---

18. Eillie Anziliotti, "For Young People, Socialism Is Now More Popular Than Capitalism," August 13, 2018, https://tinyurl.com/yb46ms3y.

gets what stuff when.[19] Within this system, a small minority privately owns what humanity needs to produce the things necessary for life—such as farms, factories, office buildings, digital servers, and intellectual property. In contrast, the vast majority must work a job and earn wages to buy the things needed to live—such as food, clothing, housing, medical care, and transportation. This is the rest of us—colloquially, the "99 percent."[20] Broadly, capitalism divides people in terms of the superior "haves" (the wealthy) and the inferior "have nots" (the rest).

The economic realities of class in the US are obscured by, among many things, two cultural myths. The first is that the majority are middle class. Dividing people under capitalism into two categories, the rich and the rest, owners and workers, is contrary to how the vast majority of US Americans identify.[21] Most, regardless of their income level or how wealthy they are,[22] want to be seen as solidly in the middle. There is tremendous shame in US American culture associated with being poor. This cultural focus on being middle class obscures the economic reality that inequality in the United States continues to climb to record levels. Significant sections of the US population represent the white supremacist and patriarchal ideals of race and gender as "white" and "male." Slightly less than half of the US population is male.[23] Slightly more than half, about 62 percent, of the US population is white.[24] However, the class ideal of the "wealthy" is an extremely small percentage of the population.

The US middle class is increasingly disappearing, a trend that has been growing since the 1980s and has accelerated in the past decade in the

19. I'm grateful to Chris Caruso with the Kairos Center for Religions, Rights, and Social Justice for this apt definition.

20. For a theological take on this contemporary rhetoric of the 1 percent and the 99 percent to describe class divisions, see Joerg Rieger and Kwok Pui-lan, *Occupy Religion: Theology of the Multitude* (Lanham, MD: Rowman & Littlefield, 2012).

21. Emmie Martin, "70% of Americans Consider Themselves Middle Class—but Only 50% Are," CNBC, June 30, 2017, https://tinyurl.com/yxzpzs6a.

22. There is an important distinction between wealth and income when addressing issues of inequality. "Income" is, for the majority, one's paycheck, the wages or salary one earns. Income can also refer to "interest on a savings account, dividends from shares of stock, rent, and profits from selling something for more than you paid for it" ("Income Inequality," Inequality.org, https://tinyurl.com/yarsyog5). In contrast, "wealth" is all of one's assets after subtracting one's liabilities. "Assets can include everything from an owned personal residence and cash in savings accounts to investments in stocks and bonds, real estate, and retirement accounts. Liabilities cover what a household owes: a car loan, credit card balance, student loan, mortgage, or any other bill yet to be paid" ("Wealth Inequality in the United States," Inequality.org, https://tinyurl.com/y8p9ry5c). This distinction between wealth and income inequality is worth noting because the majority of US Americans do not have access to substantial wealth. Wealth inequality is even more pronounced than income inequality in the US.

23. United States Census Bureau, "Age and Sex Composition: 2010," 2, https://tinyurl.com/zl8qxc6.

24. "Race and Ethnicity in the United States," Statistical Atlas, https://tinyurl.com/y4pya5za.

wake of the Great Recession of 2008.[25] The top quintile, the wealthiest 20 percent of US Americans, currently controls fully 90 percent of the country's wealth.[26] Breaking down this number further demonstrates an extreme concentration of wealth. Within this wealthiest 20 percent, 1 percent controls 40 percent of the nation's wealth. The next 4 percent own 27 percent, and the next 5 percent own another 12 percent. The bottom 40 percent of US Americans have no wealth at all and significant debt.[27] These differences among US Americans are not among the rich, the middle class, and the poor but between the ultra-wealthy and the rest, who are becoming increasingly poor. This trend is fueled not only by inequality but also by the technological innovation of automation in which many jobs humans once did are now being replaced by machines.[28] These structural shifts in the economy have created a level of precarity in which even those who identify as "professionals" or "upper middle class" can easily, for example, be one medical bankruptcy away from poverty.[29]

Related to this identification as middle class, another cultural myth that obscures the economic realities of the US is that of class mobility. US Americans are told from early childhood that anyone, if they just work hard enough, if they just pull up relentlessly enough on their proverbial "bootstraps," can become millionaires. The promise of class mobility under capitalism is different than white supremacy or patriarchy in that the vast majority will not change their skin color or gender. Yet the myth of economic mobility suggests that if a person is born poor, she is, with hard work, able to change her circumstances. US Americans are enamored of "rags to riches" stories because they perpetuate the idea that if a person does not achieve the "American dream," it is not the fault of the economic system but of the person herself. Despite the culturally embedded idea that only hard work is necessary to become successful, the economic reality suggests something quite different. According to researchers from Stanford University's Center on Poverty and Inequality, the income of one's parents largely determines one's economic future

25. Patrick Watson, "The Middle Class Might Nearly Disappear in the Next Decade," *Forbes*, March 8, 2018, https://tinyurl.com/y6gvucfr.

26. Christopher Ingraham, "The Richest 1 Percent Now Owns More of the Country's Wealth Than at Any Time in the Past 50 Years," *The Washington Post*, December 6, 2017, https://tinyurl.com/yy6d9d6p.

27. Ingraham, "Richest 1 Percent."

28. For an in-depth analysis of the impact of automation on employment, see Willie Baptist, *It's Not Enough to Be Angry* (New York: University of the Poor Press, 2015).

29. David U. Himmelstein et al., "Medical Bankruptcy in the United States, 2007: Results of a National Study," *The American Journal of Medicine* 122, no. 8 (August 2009): 741–46, https://tinyurl.com/y2a6uu6l.

from generation to generation. The results of one study "show that children born into lower-income families can expect very different futures relative to those from higher-income families" in that their circumstances will largely remain the same.[30] The majority of children born into poor families will remain poor during their lifetimes, while the majority of children born wealthy will remain wealthy.

Poverty as Structural

In light of capitalism as an ideology of oppression, I will focus on a few methodological issues about how poverty is understood in US society broadly as well as how it will be treated in this volume specifically.

Stereotypes about poverty (who are the poor, and why are they poor?) abound in US society. While assumptions have evolved historically, one stereotype today is that of an African American man without a home dressed in rags walking the streets of a city with observable mental health issues. Poverty in the US context is stereotyped as a problem particularly for people of color. The recent opioid epidemic, which has disproportionately affected poor whites,[31] has shifted this stereotype somewhat, recalling the poor Appalachian whites representative of Lyndon Johnson's 1960s "War on Poverty." Another historical stereotype popularized by Ronald Reagan was that of the "welfare queen," the African American single mother with multiple children who drives a Cadillac despite an aversion to work because she has committed welfare fraud. (The mirror opposite of this stereotype is the absent, possibly incarcerated, African American father.) The legacy of the welfare queen is evoked today by stoking the xenophobic fear of immigrants, especially from Latin America, who purportedly come to the US to have "anchor babies" and live off the welfare system. These stereotypes betray moral associations with poverty. People who are poor are seen as "lazy," "undeserving," and "undisciplined" because of an unwillingness to work, drug addiction, an inability to budget and manage financial resources, and/or because they have too many children. Race, gender, and class combine to create multiple levels of marginalization and oppression, especially with the additional layer of morality that seeks to shame people who are poor.

Cultural stereotypes about poverty often underpin the rationales scholars provide for why people are poor. One framework for under-

30. Pew Charitable Trusts and the Russell Sage Foundation, "Economic Mobility in the United States," 2, https://tinyurl.com/y4qnq38f.
31. Helena Hansen and Julie Netherland, "Is the Prescription Opioid Epidemic a White Problem?" *American Journal of Public Health* 106, no. 12 (December 2016): 2127–29.

standing the causes of poverty is Blakely and Goldsmith's "theories of impoverishment." To briefly summarize: poverty as "pathology" blames the poor for their own poverty, stating that their poverty results from psychological and behavioral deficiencies, which can create a "culture of poverty."[32] This theory places the "fault" of poverty clearly on people who are poor themselves and relates to the most blatant cultural stereotypes about laziness, stupidity, addiction, and so on. These stereotypes especially intersect with racial stereotypes about people of color as oversexed and emotional.

Poverty as "accident" or "incident" assumes people become poor because they were in the wrong place at the wrong time, and that temporary poverty will soon be replaced by the ability to meet one's basic needs.[33] With this theory, poverty is not the "fault" of a particular individual or group. For example, millennials as a generation cannot be "blamed" for coming of age and entering the job market during the Great Recession.

A third theory, added by Liz Theoharis and others at the Kairos Center for Religions, Rights, and Social Justice, is that poverty is one's "fate" or is willed by God. Jesus in the Gospels is quoted as saying "you always have the poor with you" (Matt 26:11; Mark 14:7; John 12:8). Alongside other biblical passages and theological justifications, "poverty as fate" declares that poverty is willed by God, a spiritual discipline or even a virtue.[34] Each of these theories, poverty as pathology, accident, and fate, are expressed not only in popular culture but also in public policy and academia. They influence not only how biblical scholars and economic historians interpret poverty in the ancient world but also how poverty is understood today.

32. William W. Goldsmith and Edward J. Blakely, *Separate Societies: Poverty and Inequality in U.S. Cities* (Philadelphia: Temple University Press, 1992), 4–5. For an example of a scholar employing the "poverty as pathology" theory see Dominic Rathbone, "Poverty and Population in Roman Egypt," in *Poverty in the Roman World*, ed. Margaret Atkins and Robin Osborne (New York: Cambridge University Press, 2006), 106. Rathbone assumes that a "destitute and criminal underclass" is more likely to steal than other segments of society, which pathologizes the poor. I am indebted to staff at the Kairos Center for Religions, Rights, and Social Justice for first introducing me to these theories.

33. Goldsmith and Blakely, *Separate Societies*, 6–7. For an example of a scholar employing the "poverty as accident/incident" theory, see Robin Osborne, introduction to Atkins and Osborne, eds., *Poverty in the Roman World*, 5. Osborne assumes that the "able-bodied" can subsist in periods of relative abundance, and that times of scarcity, such as those caused by drought or war, are only temporary "accidents/incidents." Aside from the fact that Osborne does not define what he means by "able-bodied," his approach assumes that there is nothing inherently poverty-producing about the Roman imperial economy. Instead he suggests that most people are able to meet their basic needs most of the time.

34. Liz Theoharis, *Always with Us? What Jesus Really Said about the Poor* (Grand Rapids: Eerdmans, 2017), 15–29.

In contrast to these three rationales, Goldsmith and Blakely's theory of poverty as "structure" argues that poverty is the result of "large-scale socioeconomic arrangements" that are inherently poverty-producing.[35] Poverty as pathology and poverty as accident both assume the economy is structured in such a way that, if people just try hard enough, they will be successful. The economic system itself is not at "fault." What distinguishes poverty as structure, however, is that it places the cause of poverty squarely on the economic structure itself, not the individuals or groups that have to live and work within it. Although a minority might understand poverty as the result of political and economic structures, many today understand poverty as the fault of the poor themselves, a mere accident of the economy, or indeed willed by God. Consequently, capitalist ideology conditions people to see poverty as something to be avoided, or even dangerous and pathological. However, on the basis of the above analysis, I argue that poverty is indeed the result of the capitalist economy. Poverty is not the result of an accident or glitch in the economic structure but rather the economy itself being inherently poverty-producing.

In the wake of growing inequality and a lack of class mobility, the majority are becoming increasingly poor. The poverty rate published by the US Census Bureau in 2017 was 12.3 percent, which included 39.7 million people. While this might seem relatively low, consider that the "poverty threshold" for a family of four (two adults, two children) that determines this rate in 2017 was a yearly income of $24,858.[36] This assessment of the amount on which a family of four can theoretically survive is extremely low compared to actual costs of living.[37] Even if poverty were measured by a standard that more closely reflected the realities in the US, using the definitions provided by the US Census Bureau, *half of US Americans are poor or low-income*.[38] Poverty is therefore not only the isolated experience of a few people who are street homeless in the "inner city." Poverty is not only the experience of people living in rural areas overcome by the opioid epidemic. Poverty is not only

35. Goldsmith and Blakely, *Separate Societies*, 8–10.
36. United States Census Bureau, "Poverty Thresholds by Size of Family and Number of Children," https://tinyurl.com/y8kvngqb.
37. The Federal Poverty Level (FPL) is based on a model developed in the 1960s that assumes a family spends one-third of its income on food. This model does not account for the additional expenses families have been burdened with over recent decades, such as rising healthcare and education costs. Other measures of poverty, such as the Census Bureau's Supplemental Poverty Measure, are more expansive and take into account additional factors such as work and child-care expenses and tax policies.
38. Paul Buchheit, "Yes, Half of Americans Are In or Near Poverty: Here's More Evidence," *Common Dreams*, October 16, 2017, https://tinyurl.com/yy9b7vwe.

the experience of people living in so-called "third world" countries in Africa, Asia, and Latin America. Poverty is as American as apple pie. What makes it so difficult to see and interpret is that capitalism (like white supremacy and patriarchy) is deeply embedded within US American society. Likewise, there is a tremendous amount of cultural shame associated with poverty that silences and isolates people from sharing from their own experiences.

Intersectionality

Before moving on to responses to these ideologies of oppression, I will briefly address the issues of intersectionality and internalized oppression. Above I alluded to the fact that race, gender, and class are not "pure" categories in that it is almost impossible to provide examples of one category without it overlapping with another. The ideologies of white supremacy, patriarchy, and capitalism intertwine with one another in intricate ways characterized by the term *intersectionality*. Intersectionality is the "complex and cumulative way that the effects of different forms of discrimination (such as racism, sexism, and classism) combine, overlap, and, yes, intersect—especially in the experiences of marginalized people or groups."[39] For example, a black man who is a business owner may be considered superior within the black community because of his economic status and gender but inferior among white colleagues within the business community because of his race. Or, as a white, cisgender woman with US citizenship at a mainline Protestant seminary, I have a very different social position than an indigenous, Latino, queer man who is in the US undocumented and working as a day laborer. In the words of Audre Lorde, "There is no such thing as a single-issue struggle because we do not live single-issue lives."[40] Intersectionality demonstrates that while white supremacy, patriarchy, and capitalism can be treated separately for the sake of theoretical clarity, in everyday reality they intersect with one another in overlapping ways.

Internalized Oppression

While the paragraphs above focus on the ways in which oppression is experienced as something external, as something that happens "to" individuals and groups, it is also important to acknowledge the ways

39. "Intersectionality," *Merriam-Webster Dictionary Online*, https://tinyurl.com/y5cnukpm.
40. Audre Lorde, *Sister Outsider: Essays and Speeches* (Berkley: Crossing, 1984), 138.

in which oppression is experienced "within" individuals and groups. Although it is not in their self-interest to do so, people who are oppressed are often those who most vehemently defend the very systems that oppress them. Audre Lorde writes,

> If our history has taught us anything, it is that action for change directed only against the external conditions of our oppressions is not enough. In order to be whole, we must recognize the despair oppression plants within each of us—that thin persistent voice that says our efforts are useless, it will never change, so why bother, accept it. And we must fight that inserted piece of self-destruction that lives and flourishes like a poison inside of us, unexamined until it makes us turn upon ourselves and each other. But we can put our finger down upon that loathing buried deep within each one of us and see who it encourages us to despise, and we can lessen its potency by the knowledge of our real connectedness, arcing across our differences.[41]

For example, under white supremacy, people of color may experience internalized racism by trying to "pass" as white or trying to change their appearance to look white. Under patriarchy, a mother-in-law will criticize a daughter-in-law for a lack of conformity to patriarchal values as a traditional wife and mother. Despite being exploited by his boss, a worker will often defend the capitalist system in the hopes that one day he too will be able to own a business and employ his own workers. Recognizing the role of internalized oppression means understanding how ideologies of oppression are experienced not only externally but also internally in one's relationship to oneself and others.

While each ideology of oppression has been explored in brief, it is important to acknowledge that these ways through which people are conditioned to see the world for many are largely unexamined and even normative. Returning to the metaphor from *The Matrix*, ideologies of oppression are phenomena that cannot be touched, tasted, or seen without developing an awareness of how they function in everyday life. They are deeply embedded within the root systems not only of US American society but, for that matter, of Western civilization. To begin to see things differently starts with developing a conscious awareness of these ideologies.

This process of seeing differently is not far removed from the Greek word *apocalypsis*, from which the English "apocalypse" is derived. While "apocalypse" typically inspires fiery images of the end of the world, its origin suggests something different. The Greek *apocalypsis* is drawn

---

41. Lorde, *Sister Outsider*, 142.

from the verb *kalupto*, which means "to cover" or "conceal";[42] and the nouns *kalux*, which means "shell" or "bud";[43] *kalumma*, which is a "cover" or "veil";[44] and *apo*, which, as a preposition of separation, can mean "away" or "from."[45] Taken together, an *apocalypsis* is an "uncovering" or an "unveiling."[46] It is the ability to see what was previously hidden, or to see beyond or past what obscures reality. Building on this derivation of *apocalypsis*, if a bud blooms, one has the ability to see the previously "hidden" flower. Or if a woman lifts her veil, her face, which was previously covered, can be seen. The process of increasing awareness, what in movement contexts is sometimes called political education and leadership development, and in black parlance "becoming woke," is exactly this type of "lifting the veil" on the ideologies of oppression. One individual and collective response to this growing awareness of oppression is the struggle for liberation.

THE CATEGORY OF STRUGGLE

Exploring ideologies of oppression broadly, and poverty specifically, requires a different way of seeing. Suggesting alternative forms of ideological formation does not imply neutrality. These forms are contested terrain. To engage in ideological formation "from below"—to learn how to see differently from the perspective of the oppressed rather than the oppressor—means coming into conflict with the ideologies of oppression imposed "from above."

The struggle is first to become aware that ideologies of oppression exist and notice the ways in which they function in one's individual and collective life. To struggle is to recognize that some people in the US, on account of their race, gender, and class, have to fight for their dignity and humanity to be recognized, while some do not. It is to recognize that some people are seen as "deserving" of the human rights to health, housing, a living wage, and a clean environment, while others are deemed "undeserving." Noticing the ways in which oppressive ideologies function, the ways in which human thriving, or even survival, is limited by these beliefs, enables people to begin to acknowledge the need for liberation.

42. Henry George Liddell and Robert Scott, "καλύπτω," *A Greek-English Lexicon* (Oxford: Clarendon, 1996), 871.

43. Liddell and Scott, "κάλυξ," *Greek-English Lexicon*, 871.

44. Liddell and Scott, "κάλυμμα," *Greek-English Lexicon*, 871.

45. Liddell and Scott, "ἀπό," *Greek-English Lexicon*, 191–92.

46. Liddell and Scott, "ἀποκάλυψις," *Greek-English Lexicon*, 201.

The struggle, then, is to seek liberation from the interlocking ideologies of white supremacy, patriarchy, and capitalism and to fundamentally dismantle these ideologies. Some people have no choice but to struggle, survive, and make ends meet from day to day. But there is a difference between the struggle to make ends meet, to stay alive, and the conscious struggle for liberation. Granted, these struggles often intersect.

The struggle then is a movement from implicitly seeing the world through the hierarchies of whites over people of color, men over women, and owners over workers to putting individual and collective practices in place that create relationships of mutuality and solidarity.[47] This struggle has been unfolding for generations and will need to continue for generations in order to come to realization. Liberation is a vision in which difference is not a tool of oppression but a celebration of diversity, in which the dignity of every human being is respected and held sacred.

There are many ways to approach the struggle for social, political, and economic change—individual activism; participation in social justice and movement organizations, in faith communities, in political education and leadership development, in community organizing, and in organizing on social media platforms; and advocating for policy change at the local, state, and national levels. Many of these approaches overlap with one another. (Some also see supporting political parties as a path to change, although my own experience has convinced me that work at the grassroots is more transformative for the long haul.) Organizations will often use several tools in the "movement toolbox" simultaneously.

While this volume is rooted in the experience of social movements, it would be a book in itself to write about the "theories of change" that underpin them. The specific form of struggle that informs this book, and to which I am personally committed, is embeddedness within grassroots social movement organizations led by those most directly impacted by the issues they seek to change. Those who know most intimately the ways in which US American society needs to change can help everyone collectively learn what is needed to change it. To borrow a phrase from the Shackdwellers Movement Abahlali baseMjondolo in South Africa, "Struggle is a school."[48] It is in communities of the organized poor that people working for change learn what they need. In a methodology of

---

47. This language of the movement from hierarchical to horizontal relationships is rooted in Brigitte Kahl's empire-critical reading of Galatians and, by extension, the undisputed Pauline corpus. For the exegetical basis of this movement toward relationships of "One-an(d)-Otherness," see Kahl, *Galatians Re-Imagined*, 265–85.

48. Richard Pithouse, "Struggle Is a School: The Rise of the Shackdwellers' Movement in Durban, South Africa," *Monthly Review* 57, no. 9 (February 1, 2006): 30–51.

reading the Bible with the poor, the struggle is the social location from which reading the Bible is learned.

A Commitment to Communities of the Organized Poor

In the tradition of Contextual Bible Study, reading the Bible is first about where your hands and feet are. The struggle is about a commitment to embeddedness within and accountability to specific communities of the organized poor, and it is out of work with these communities that reading the Bible with the poor flows. In the words of Gustavo Gutiérrez in the seminal *A Theology of Liberation*, "Theology is reflection, a critical attitude. Theology *follows*; it is the second step. What Hegel used to say about philosophy can likewise be applied to theology: it rises only at sundown. The pastoral activity of the Church does not flow as a conclusion from theological premises. Theology does not produce pastoral activity; rather it reflects upon it."[49] In this tradition, reading the Bible with the poor is likewise a second step. It is a reflection of work that is already underway and of relationships already being built.

In this volume "the poor" is not a rhetorical category, an illustration of a phenomenon, an indiscriminate, anonymous mass of people, or a stock photo. I do not refer to "the poor" in general but to specific people who are both poor and organizing to transform their lived reality. Therefore, in the following chapters I refer to specific groups as concrete examples of organizations under the leadership of those directly impacted by the issues they seek to change.

In recognition of not treating "the poor" or even "communities of the organized poor" in the abstract, it is also important not to romanticize or idealize "the struggle" or specific poor people's organizations. The work that happens in social movement organizations can be beautiful, inspiring, and even breathtaking. It can also be brutal, transactional, and hypocritical. Social movement organizations often replicate many of the same ideologies of oppression they seek to transform through practices of workaholism, time discipline, accountability to funding structures like corporate foundations that can compromise and co-opt the work, and micro- and macroaggressions rooted in unexamined racism, patriarchy, and classism. Gerald West points out,

> As José Míguez-Bonino said to us when he visited us in South Africa shortly after our liberation (in 1994), we have to do careful and detailed analysis of

49. Gustavo Gutiérrez, *A Theology of Liberation: History, Politics, and Salvation*, trans. and ed. Caridad Inda and John Eagleson, rev. ed. (Maryknoll, NY: Orbis, 1988).

received concepts such as "the poor." He reflected, sadly, that the solidarity amongst the poor and other marginalised sectors could no longer be taken for granted. The "new poor," he said, preyed on each other instead of standing with each other. . . . For some, the poor and marginalised are or have become ideologically co-opted and corrupted, requiring a more directly interventionist orientation from the (organically) socially engaged "scholarly" reader. However, even those who emphasise the "false consciousness" of the poor and marginalised would not question that they are the primary site of liberation hermeneutics.[50]

The specific experiences of social movement organizations are full of both beauty and grit.

It is out of concrete work together with communities of the organized poor that biblical scholars might be "invited to participate in Bible reading with local communities."[51] It is from this place that the Bible might become a resource in the struggle for liberation.

The Bible as a Resource for Struggle

Before moving into the specific methodological considerations of reading the Bible with the poor, I will clarify what I mean by "the Bible." For me, the Bible is a product of history held sacred and passed down by faithful communities across the centuries. I recognize that the majority of the communities with which I work do not interpret the Bible in this way. I have encountered a range of perspectives about the authority of the Bible. Some believe the Bible is the totally inerrant Word of God dictated by the Holy Spirit into the ears of faithful scribes. Some see it only as a collection of stories. For me, it is a library of books written, revised, and collected over several centuries by communities of faith that were first Jewish and later Christian in the centuries that followed the writing of the New Testament. The canonical Hebrew Scriptures and New Testament are the result of human choices, negotiations, and politics through which God has continued to speak. As just one brief example, the early church did not decide on a list of books it considered authoritative until the fourth century CE, hundreds of years after the earthly ministry of Jesus the Christ. Naming the Bible as a product of history makes it no less sacred to me than to those who may view the Bible through "uncritical" or "ahistorical" lenses. In fact, that liberating

50. Gerald O. West, "Locating Contextual Bible Study within Biblical Liberation Hermeneutics and Intercultural Biblical Hermeneutics," *Theological Studies* 70, no. 1 (2014): https://tinyurl.com/yyxkeque.

51. Gerald O. West, *The Academy of the Poor: Towards a Dialogical Reading of the Bible* (Sheffield: Sheffield Academic, 1999), 18.

voices could continue to speak in the Bible through the flawed, broken realities of humanity, for me, makes it all the more sacred.

As a product of history, the Bible is not neutral. As a reflection of its time, the Bible is inherently patriarchal and shaped by the empires of antiquity. The Bible is not ideologically consistent, and it does not speak with one voice. It is a collage of voices and perspectives accumulated over centuries, some representing the voices of the powerful, those who sought to defend the status quo, and some representing voices of those who sought to challenge and transform the powers and principalities.

While I claim the Bible as a story of liberation, it is important to acknowledge how the Bible, perhaps predominantly and for the majority of its history, has been used in the hands of the church and other institutions of power to justify and supplement ideologies of oppression. The church has historically played, and still today often plays, a role in maintaining the status quo. In the hands of the church, "The temptation is to force the Bible to fit the perspective we have inherited. Yet a Bible which must 'fit' a perspective is not one that is going to tell us anything new. It becomes an ideological weapon in our defense of our own version of the status quo."[52] The Bible has been weaponized from the founding of the US to support the genocide of the First Nations and enslavement of Africans. It has been used to deny women civil and political rights, including the right to vote. It has been used to uphold capitalist values of hard work and self-sufficiency to the detriment of the health and well-being of workers. The legacies of these historical traumas continue to play out in US American society.

The Bible has left concrete and specific wounds on the individual and collective bodies, minds, and spirits of people in the US. As a small example, when I was an undergraduate discerning a call to ministry, my boyfriend at the time quoted me 1 Timothy 2:12 as if it were obvious that women should keep quiet because they do not have the authority to teach. A person shared with me the experience of his father quoting the Bible as his father ruthlessly beat him as a child. Over and over in the broader culture and in social movement contexts poverty is named as inevitable, indeed perhaps even a gift from God, because "you always have the poor with you" (Matt 26:11). Yet God sent God's Child into the world so that we might have life and have it abundantly (John 10:10). Miguel A. De La Torre argues,

---

52. David Lochhead, "The Liberation of the Bible," in *The Bible and Liberation: Political and Social Hermeneutics*, ed. Norman K. Gottwald and Richard A. Horsley, rev. ed. (Maryknoll, NY: Orbis, 1993), 132.

If a biblical interpretation prevents life from being lived abundantly by a segment of the population or, worse, if it brings death, then it is anti-gospel. When a reading of the Bible ignores how minority groups are denied access to opportunities, when the Bible is read to rationalize the riches of the center while disregarding the plight of the poor, and when reading the Bible vindicates the relegation of women to second-class status, then such interpretations cease to be biblically based. Only interpretations that empower all elements of humanity, offering abundant life in the here-now, as opposed to just the here-after, are biblically sound.[53]

Whenever the Bible is used as a bludgeon, as a weapon to support white supremacy, patriarchy, or capitalism, it is a sin against God and one's neighbor.

Acknowledging the weight of this history and the need for ongoing confession of sin and repentance, I argue that new life is still possible and that the Bible can indeed be used as a theological resource for liberation. It is only with a tremendous sense of responsibility and care that the Bible can be taken up in this way. While the Bible speaks with a multiplicity of voices, many of which are oppressive, and is written from many perspectives, I agree with Wes Howard-Brook that there is an arc narrative that grounds the biblical story from Genesis to Revelation into which all of God's people are invited.

The Bible does not present a single, unified perspective on what it means to be a "Jew" or a "Christian." Rather, it gathers together witnesses to a passionate, historical argument over what it means to be "God's people." It constantly keeps before its audience questions that must be wrestled with before our central question can even be addressed. "Which 'god' are you talking about? Which 'side' are you on?" The Bible insists that there are no "sidelines" from which to watch others do battle. All people are inevitably and unavoidably drawn into the fray, or at least its consequences, by the fact of sharing this beautiful, abundant, yet fragile and finite planet as our home. We can choose to run away, to be silent, or to hide, but we cannot choose not to participate.[54]

The Bible is ultimately a story of the movement from slavery to freedom, of the passage from the powers of sin and death to liberation and life, and of the need to continually discern on which side of death and slavery or life and freedom one stands.

The evidence for this liberating strand within the Bible is borne out

---

53. Miguel A. De La Torre, *Reading the Bible from the Margins* (Maryknoll, NY: Orbis, 2002), 54.

54. Wes Howard-Brook, *"Come Out, My People!": God's Call Out of Empire in the Bible and Beyond* (Maryknoll, NY: Orbis, 2010), 4.

by how it has been taken by those who have struggled for freedom in the US context. Michelle Alexander points out that "the whole of American history can be described as a struggle between those who truly embraced the revolutionary idea of freedom, equality, and justice for all and those who resisted."[55] Throughout this history the Bible has been used as a resource to challenge, transform, legitimize, and dialogue with historic and contemporary struggles for liberation from the abolitionist movement to end slavery,[56] to the women's suffrage movement,[57] and to the civil rights movement.[58] Each of these movements has recognized and lifted up the resonances between their own struggles for freedom and the strands of liberation found in the Bible.

The stories of liberation in the Bible have the potential to become dialogue partners with (post)modern stories of liberation. Here is an example of how the strands of Bible stories and movement stories can intertwine. As a graduate student Richard A. Horsley, now a prominent biblical scholar, was organizing with a housing project in the Boston area. He found himself at the kitchen table of "the very elderly Mrs. Brimmage," to whom he listened "spell-bound as she narrated the Exodus story, shifting seamlessly back and forth from Moses's time to her grandfather's experience under slavery, and to the events of the 1960s."[59] *The Gospel of Solentiname* is another example of this type of interweaving from Central America. Over a period of four years in the 1970s, Catholic priest Ernesto Cardenal read the Bible with *campesinos* ("peasants") struggling against the Somoza dictatorship in Nicaragua and transcribed the group's conversations before the community was destroyed by the army

55. Michelle Alexander, "We Are Not the Resistance," *The New York Times*, September 21, 2018, https://tinyurl.com/y77ugonw.

56. For examples of biblical interpretation in light of the abolitionist movement against US American slavery, see Margaret P. Aymer, *First Pure, Then Peaceable: Frederick Douglass, Darkness and the Epistle of James* (London: T&T Clark, 2008); and Emerson B. Powery and Rodney S. Sadler Jr., *The Genesis of Liberation: Biblical Interpretation in the Antebellum Narratives of the Enslaved* (Louisville: Westminster John Knox, 2016).

57. For examples of biblical interpretation in light of the women's suffrage movement in the United States, see Katie Geneva Cannon, *Katie's Canon: Womanism and the Soul of the Black Community* (New York: Continuum, 1995); Elizabeth Cady Stanton, *The Woman's Bible* (New York: Arno, 1972); and Marion Ann Taylor and Agnes Choi, eds., *Handbook of Women Biblical Interpreters: A Historical and Biographical Guide* (Grand Rapids: Baker Academic, 2012).

58. While there were many pastors and preachers among the leaders of the civil rights movement, one of the most prominent examples is Martin Luther King Jr., whose speeches and writings are threaded with biblical language. See Martin Luther King Jr., *A Testament of Hope: The Essential Writings of Martin Luther King Jr.*, ed. James Melvin Washington (San Francisco: HarperSanFrancisco, 1991).

59. Noelle Damico, "The Intellectual and Social Impact of an Engaged Scholar: Richard A. Horsley's Legacy," in *Bridges in New Testament Interpretation: Interdisciplinary Advances*, ed. Neil Elliott and Werner H. Kelber (New York: Lexington, 2018), 257.

and Cardenal was himself forced into exile in Costa Rica.[60] As a story ultimately of liberation, the Bible has historically been and can continue to be claimed as a theological resource in the ongoing struggle for liberation.

Having addressed in a preliminary way how the Bible has been used in the US context as both a tool of oppression and a resource for liberation, it almost goes without saying that the Bible is contested terrain. But regardless of whether one is a person of faith or a person of no faith, the language and stories of the Bible permeate US culture. There is a choice therefore in whether to claim the Bible as a resource for liberation and life or whether to cede the Bible to those who would use it to continue to justify oppression. It is from a place with the weight of this history and within this US context that the invitation to read the Bible with the poor can come.

The "Call to Conversion"

After engaging in work and developing relationships with communities of the organized poor, an invitation may come to the "trained reader" to read the Bible with one of these communities. I use the term "trained reader" in the spirit in which it has been articulated by West and the Contextual Bible Study tradition of the "socially engaged biblical scholar."[61] This type of scholar stands in contrast to the majority of mainstream biblical scholars in the US American context who have historically reflected and continue to reflect today commitments that are white, male, cisgender, and heterosexual, and perceived as middle to upper class professionals because of their education. These scholars occupy positions of relative privilege and social power and mostly do not seek to dismantle these relative privileges and powers. However, with the advent of the women's rights, civil rights, and gay rights movements, biblical scholars are becoming increasingly diverse. The profession of biblical scholarship, however, is by no means representative of the US population broadly, which is becoming increasingly heterogeneous in terms of race, ethnicity, nationality, and language. It has been less than a century since the voices of women and people of color entered mainstream biblical scholarship, and white men continue to dominate membership in the Society of Biblical Literature, the professional association of biblical scholars. Membership in the Society of Biblical Literature is currently about 70

---

60. Ernesto Cardenal, introduction to *The Gospel of Solentiname*, trans. Donald D. Walsh (Maryknoll, NY: Orbis, 1976), xiv.

61. West, *Academy of the Poor*, 46–62.

percent male and 85 percent white.[62] Ironically, while Jesus himself was a poor person of color living under Rome, effectively feminine in gender as a member of a conquered people,[63] the voices of people living in poverty continue to be almost entirely excluded from biblical interpretation.

While traditionally a biblical scholar with formal academic training, I treat the category of "trained reader" flexibly in that this person might also be a pastor, social worker, or community organizer with formal or informal training. The trained reader may or may not have institutional recognition through an academic institution, church, or another type of organization. The trained reader typically has a level of educational and social privilege that, in reading with communities of the organized poor, is important to acknowledge and decenter to the extent this decentering is possible. I will address these issues in more detail in the facilitation chapter. For the purposes of this volume, I will use "trained reader" and "biblical scholar" interchangeably, recognizing there a number of different roles in addition to the biblical scholar that a trained reader might play.

Embeddedness within organized struggles and the invitation to read the Bible with communities of the organized poor may create increasing orientation toward their voices, perspectives, and questions. The work becomes an appropriation of the category of "struggle" as the lens through which the Bible is interpreted.[64] Reading the Bible through the lens of struggle can begin to shift one's primary formation in oppressive ideologies toward a different way of seeing. This willingness to betray one's primary formation through being partially constituted by the perspective of the organized poor is a "call to conversion."

The Ujamaa Centre, based at the University of KwaZulu-Natal in Pietermaritzburg, South Africa, recognizes two moments of conversion. The first time one is converted, the moment in which one becomes a Christian, is "from above." But the second time is a conversion "from below." As West rightly notes, "Use of the term *conversion* is not simply for dramaturgical effect; to be of use to others is not easy, it is difficult. Offering ourselves and our resources may be costly, choosing collaboration instead of conversation may be painful, and participating in

62. Society of Biblical Literature, "2018 SBL Membership Report," https:// tinyurl.com/ y25vpjvo.

63. For an in-depth treatment of the gender construction of conquered peoples under the Roman empire and its implications for biblical interpretation, see Davina Lopez, *Apostle to the Conquered: Reimagining Paul's Mission* (Minneapolis: Fortress, 2008).

64. Osayande Obrey Hendricks, "Guerrilla Exegesis: 'Struggle' as a Scholarly Vocation: A Postmodern Approach to African-American Biblical Interpretation," *Semeia* 72 (1995): 73–90.

a reading process that is often eclectic and strategic may be disturbing. So we do need to be converted."[65] Although described here as two moments, conversion to the perspectives of the organized poor and reading the Bible through the lens of struggle is an ongoing process.[66] The biblical scholar must recommit herself over and over to being partially constituted by this perspective, especially because this perspective conflicts with the ideological assumptions of the status quo in which she has been formed. Conversion is a process toward one perspective and away from another. It is a challenging and betraying of one type of ideological formation in favor of another through ongoing accountability to communities of the organized poor.

What Is the Role of "Betrayal"?

Similar except in class position to the mainstream biblical scholar, the ideal of each of the intersecting systems of oppression is a straight, cis-gender, white, owning class male. Patriarchy, white supremacy, and capitalism are built on addiction to being rewarded by these systems. There can be a high that comes with conforming. It feels good to do what is expected of oneself, to be "normal," to the extent that is possible based on one's identity. There is potentially wealth and social status to be gained in constructing the "Self" with a capital "S" over and against the "Others" who are seen as "less than" and excluded. An unwillingness to conform to these ideological systems involves certain levels of betrayal depending on one's position within these intersecting systems. For example, middle and upper class, well-educated, heterosexual white men have quite a bit more at stake in giving up their relative privilege than poor, uneducated, trans women of color. The higher one "rises" or is affirmed by ideologies of oppression, the farther one has to "fall."

White supremacy, patriarchy, and capitalism have never worked for people who are poor, uneducated, indigenous, transgender, of color, and/or undocumented. These ideologies tend to exploit and marginalize, and may ultimately murder people with these identities. There is far less at stake for people who have little or nothing to lose under the current systems because they are far less invested in systems that have never worked for them. Someone who is affirmed by these systems has more to lose if the systems from which they benefit are transformed. For example, as a white person, I benefit from a white supremacist ideology that ultimately labels people of color as inferior, as "Other." But as a woman

65. West, *Academy of the Poor*, 34.
66. West, *Academy of the Poor*, 18.

I do not benefit from patriarchy. It is in my self-interest to transform the patriarchal system from which I do not benefit. As a worker, it is in my self-interest to transform a system that exploits my labor, to make the conditions of my labor more bearable, and ultimately to change my relationship to the economy. However, being partially constituted by the perspective of the organized poor calls one increasingly to come to recognize how one benefits from a system *at the expense of* the very people who are exploited by that same system.

People who benefit from the status quo have the most at stake in "betraying" identities associated with power, privilege, and prestige as well as the scholarly pretense of objectivity. West points out that

> usually the connection between our work as biblical scholars and our life commitments is covert, and if our work is to be used by others, we want to remain in control. But clearly the interface [among "ordinary readers" and "socially engaged biblical scholars"] . . . demands an overt connection between our biblical research and our social commitments, and that we risk allowing our work and ourselves to be used by others without our control.[67]

What I mean by "betrayal" is a willingness to align oneself, to express commitment, but more importantly, to act in concrete practices of solidarity with the "Other." People who benefit, in varying degrees, from these systems of oppression are called in reading the Bible with the organized poor to make a conscious and continual decision to be constituted by perspectives potentially different from the ones in which they were brought up. In working with people who are, for example, poor, queer, and/or of color, they risk being perceived as "guilty by association," as if to be a person of a marginalized identity is somehow a crime. Or they experience new levels of marginalization themselves. To be partially constituted by the perspectives of the organized poor, and in doing so betraying the ideologies of oppression to enforce the status quo, is inherently countercultural. It is a willingness to go against the grain, to swim upstream instead of going with the flow.

Accountability for the Sake of Liberation

Responding to the call to conversion and betraying any relative privilege can create a relationship of ongoing accountability with communities of the organized poor for the sake of liberation. While this approach to biblical interpretation might be labeled by mainstream biblical scholarship

---

67. West, *Academy of the Poor*, 34.

as "ideological" or "political," it is important to keep in mind the idea that understanding biblical criticism as an "objective" or "scientific" discipline is increasingly falling by the wayside.

There is increasing recognition within biblical studies that all readings of the Bible are political. As Walter Brueggemann rightly observes, "'Reading the Bible politically,' is something of a misnomer. It is a misnomer because all reading of the Bible is political, that is, read with dimensions of power and vested interest operative in the interpretive process."[68] The difference between so-called "political" and "objective" interpretations is that those claiming to be objective have historically been (and still are) those white, male, professional biblical scholars who maintain positions of power and privilege within the guild, while "minority" and "marginalized" perspectives have been labeled "political." Biblical studies is shaped by ideologies of oppression just as much as any other academic discipline. It interacts with them as much as it rejects them. There is increasing recognition that historical criticism, the foundation of "scientific exegesis," brings its own ideological assumptions to the biblical text. To claim "objectivity" in itself is inherently political with relative power maintained behind the guise of objectivity. Reading the Bible with the poor is a process of interpretation that is transparent about its political and ideological commitments.

Likewise, reading the Bible with the poor does not engage in interpretation for its own sake but for the sake of liberation. It places the tools of biblical scholarship at the service of movements working for social change. It does not ask movement organizers, activists, leaders, and organic intellectuals to "respond" to the work of biblical scholarship. These leaders do not function as proof of the "applicability" or the "relevance" of biblical scholarship. Rather, accountable biblical scholarship works to respond to the questions these leaders are asking. Its purpose is not to ask questions for their own sake, to legitimize the "life of the mind," or to justify the existence of a professional class of biblical scholars and theologians. No, rather it seeks to hold biblical studies accountable, to ask why it does its work in the first place, and to bring a level of intention to those questions it is trying to answer.

A lot of biblical scholars hope that their work will be "relevant," that it will somehow "trickle down" to the pews and the parishes. In some ways it does, very slowly and indirectly. Liberation theology, forty years after its advent, does get preached in some churches in the US context. Reading the Bible with the poor is an effort toward bridge-building

68. Walter Brueggemann, "Introduction: Reading the Bible Politically," in *An Eerdmans Reader in Contemporary Political Theology*, ed. William T. Cavanaugh, Jeffrey W. Baily, and Craig Hovey (Grand Rapids: Eerdmans, 2012), 4.

and "translating" work, leveraging the intellectual resources of academia toward the people with whom it seeks to dialogue through concrete practices of reading the Bible together in communities of organized struggle. In sum, "at the heart of liberation hermeneutics is the relationship between the biblical scholar (or theologian) and the ordinary Christian 'reader' from a poor and marginalized community."[69]

The Epistemological Privilege of the Poor

Unlike traditional biblical scholarship, which draws primarily from other academic disciplines like history, archeology, economics, literary criticism, and critical theory, reading the Bible with the poor creates epistemologies, specific kinds of knowledge, at the intersection of academia, including all of those disciplines, *and* the social movements of the organized poor, drawing on many different types of knowledge traditionally considered outside academia.

Beyond the traditional academic discipline of history, which has recorded the events of, for example, the abolitionist, women's suffrage, and civil rights movements, reading the Bible with the poor also draws on lineages of oral and movement histories in something akin to people's histories.[70] Related to drawing lessons from these histories for contemporary movements, other types of knowledge used by social movements include strategy and tactics. There are also the "hard skills" like facilitation, one-to-one conversations, door-knocking, canvassing, and planning and executing a variety of events from educational forums to marches to civil disobedience. Embedded within but also different from these "nuts and bolts" skills is knowledge of pedagogy, curriculum development, political education, and leadership development. Organizing is not exactly an academic discipline, but it does draw on many different types of knowledge.

Reading the Bible with the poor deliberately centers the voices, knowledges, and experiences of those in struggle, of the poor and marginalized themselves. This process privileges the knowledges specifically of the *organized* poor. It combines the "theoretical" approaches traditionally associated with biblical studies and the "practical" approaches typically associated with organizing. It is a movement toward an epistemological privileging, a process of especially valuing the particular

---

69. West, *Academy of the Poor*, 18.

70. Davina C. Lopez, "Minding the Gaps: Reflections on the Fantasy of People's History in the Study of Christian Origins," in *Bridges in New Testament Interpretation: Interdisciplinary Advances*, ed. Neil Elliott and Werner H. Kelber, 255–310 (New York: Lexington, 2018).

types of knowledge, that perspectives of the organized poor bring to the movement for liberation.[71]

The ideological and methodological considerations of this chapter might be best summarized by breaking apart the phrase "reading the Bible with the poor." Beginning at the end, I use "the poor" not as a rhetorical category but as a referent for specific communities of the organized poor engaged in struggle to transform ideologies of oppression, here specifically white supremacy, patriarchy, and capitalism. Second, "reading with" is a call to trained readers by these organized communities to an ongoing relationship of accountability. Through that relationship might come a specific invitation to read the Bible as a resource in the struggle for liberation. Lastly, "the Bible" is a product of history, a multiplicity of voices guided by the overarching story of a movement from slavery and bondage to liberation and freedom. Reading the Bible with organized communities is a second step, a reflection on practices of solidarity already underway.

The next two chapters provide examples of what this relationship of "reading with" has looked like within specific contexts in Baltimore. Chapter 2 reads the story of Naboth's vineyard in 1 Kings 21 alongside a campaign to stop the construction of the nation's largest trash-burning incinerator. Chapter 3 reads the fear and silence of the women at the "empty" tomb in Mark 16 alongside "the vacants," the most visible symbol of Baltimore's housing crisis.

---

71. Crystal L. Hall and Luis Larín, "United Workers' Model of Organizing with Faith Communities: Unity across Lines of Division," paper presented to the Annual Meeting of the Society of Biblical Literature, Baltimore, Maryland, November 22, 2013, 7–10.

2.

An Incinerator Comes to Naboth's Vineyard: 1 Kings 21:1–16

The stereotypes of Baltimore created by the dominant white culture in the US suggest a majority black city that is crime-filled, drug-infested, and to be avoided at all cost. For example, the HBO TV series *The Wire* (2002–2008) made Baltimore (in)famous by filming much of the series within the city proper, putting its most impoverished areas on display in high definition. *The Wire* portrays Baltimore as a city full of gang violence, plagued by an ineffectual police department, corrupt public officials, and a broken school system. In 2015 the national news media put Baltimore back in the spotlight during the uprising in response to the death of Freddie Gray, a young African American man, in police custody. Cable news networks played footage of a burning CVS store and street protests over and over again, contributing to an image of Baltimore as a chaotic, lawless city.

These mainstream media portrayals made it easy to assume, from an outsider's perspective, that Baltimore was a bad apple, an exception to the rule of US American prosperity. They fell squarely within racist assumptions that poverty concentrated among black and brown peoples was a result of their moral failings and pathological tendencies, caught up in an endless cycle of poverty.[1] Despite these assumptions, Baltimore was typical of many postindustrial cities, by no means an exception to the rule in terms of its political, economic, and sociocultural dynamics.

1. The stereotypes of Baltimore fit squarely within a theory of "poverty as pathology." See chapter 1 for an overview of the theories of impoverishment, and for reference to the "poverty as pathology" theory in particular, see William W. Goldsmith and Edward J. Blakely, *Separate Societies: Poverty and Inequality in U.S. Cities* (Philadelphia: Temple University Press, 1992), 4–5.

From the 1860s to the 1950s Baltimore's industrial economy boomed alongside those of many US cities.[2] After the Civil War Baltimore's most important industries were shipbuilding, canning, and cotton mills. From the 1870s to the beginning of World War I, heavy industries such as copper and steel processing were important during the second wave of industrialization. The Bethlehem Steel plant, located southeast of what is now downtown Baltimore, the largest steel plant in the world, was known as the "Beast of the East." In the 1950s Baltimore's population began steadily declining through a combination of suburbanization, white flight, and racial discrimination. Many whites fled the city for the suburbs, supported by the incentivization of home ownership in the GI Bill, and in response to an influx of African Americans moving into the city.[3] Through racist practices known as redlining, banks would only offer mortgage loans to African Americans in certain overcrowded, formerly white neighborhoods. The effects of Baltimore's declining population were compounded, beginning in the 1970s, by deindustrialization.[4] Corporations increasingly replaced unionized, family-sustaining factory jobs with precarious, low-wage service-sector jobs hostile to worker organizing. Under industrialization, profits were shared more equally between owners and workers—although by no means equitably[5]—but deindustrialization fueled growing inequality. Alongside many cities in the United States, Baltimore's poverty was the result of historical changes in a political and economic system that facilitated a few becoming increasingly rich while the majority struggled to make ends meet. It was not a result of perceived pathological or moral failings among communities of color.

One aspect of Baltimore's poverty that has largely escaped notice is its environmental factors. For example, news coverage during the 2015 uprising reported on the high levels of lead poisoning among children

2. Marilyn Kindrick Julius and Luis Larín, "Baltimore Economic Reality Tour," paper presented at the Annual Meeting of the Society of Biblical Literature, Baltimore, Maryland, November 22, 2013.

3. Julius and Larín, "Baltimore Economic Reality Tour."

4. The deindustrialization in Baltimore reflected the major structural shifts in the global economy occurring in the 1970s and 1980s with the advent of neoliberal economic policy. For an introduction to the historical development of neoliberalism, see David Harvey, *The Condition of Postmodernity: An Enquiry into the Origins of Cultural Change* (Cambridge: Blackwell, 1989).

5. There is an important distinction between equality and equity in that equality assumes everyone gets the same amount of something, such as funding, access to resources, etc. Equity, however, recognizes that because of histories of oppression, some individuals and groups need *more* resources than others because of the ways in which they have been marginalized to be equal with individuals and groups who have had privileged advantages. For more on the use of this concept in popular, movement-based education, see Paul Kuttner, "The Problem with That Equity vs. Equality Graphic You're Using," October 29, 2016, https://tinyurl.com/h4mx5nk.

in the poor neighborhoods like Sandtown-Winchester, where Freddie Gray grew up. "As populations and employment opportunities shrank in recent decades, poverty and neglect combined with older housing allowed lead paint poisoning to plague the city."[6] While not traditionally considered an environmental issue, exposure to lead is toxic in any amount, especially for young children,[7] and was just one specific example within a larger pattern of environmental injustice in Baltimore. While there has been so much focus in the national media on the city's violent crime, four times more people die every year from air pollution than homicide in Baltimore.[8] In light of the historical and more recent trends outlined above, this chapter will focus on a campaign organized in response to Baltimore's current plight, especially where poverty and the environment intersect, and the ways in which faith communities used the Bible as a resource in the struggle for clean air and a healthy environment.

The Curtis Bay neighborhood in South West Baltimore was ranked one of the most polluted zip codes in the US until 2008, when the only monitor for fine particulate matter was removed. According to the Environmental Protection Agency, fine particulate matter is a type of air pollution, "a mixture of solid particles and liquid droplets. . . . Some particles, such as dust, dirt, soot, or smoke, are large or dark enough to be seen with the naked eye. Others are so small they can only be detected using an electron microscope."[9] Without a monitor there was no way to determine the actual levels of air pollution in the area, even though they were often visible to the naked eye in the form of the dust that settled on every available surface from cars to porches.

Curtis Bay's air pollution was caused by the heavy industries that have operated there for centuries, often to the detriment of the community. In recent history, over a period of fifteen years from 1996 to 2011, the entire neighboring community of Fairfield was displaced to make way for heavy industry because the health of the community could no longer be guaranteed.[10] While the types of industry in Curtis Bay

6. Anna Maria Barry-Jester, "Baltimore's Toxic Legacy of Lead Paint," *FiveThirtyEight*, May 7, 2015, https://tinyurl.com/y5qsbu5x.

7. Centers for Disease Control and Prevention, "Childhood Lead Poisoning Data, Statistics, and Surveillance," https://tinyurl.com/y64kqhq6.

8. Maryland Environmental Health Network, "Energy & Health in Maryland: A Briefing for Health Advocates," 3, https://tinyurl.com/y6mf3vsw.

9. United States Environmental Protection Agency, "Particulate Matter (PM) Basics," https://tinyurl.com/zss3hst.

10. For environmental histories of the Curtis Bay, Fairfield, and Wagner's Point neighborhoods in southwest Baltimore, see Chloe Ahmann, "Cumulative Effects: Reckoning Risks on Baltimore's Toxic Periphery," PhD diss., The George Washington University, forthcoming,

have changed over the years, plants currently operating include a coal terminal, an animal rendering plant,[11] chemical plants, hazardous waste sites, the country's largest medical waste incinerator, and a host of other polluting industries, many of which operate in violation of the federal Clean Water and Clean Air Acts.[12] The air pollution emitted from these plants has caused a range of public health problems from increased rates of asthma to heart and respiratory disease.[13]

Despite the heavy environmental burden already placed on southwest Baltimore, in 2011 Maryland's political leaders, including then Governor Martin O'Malley and Baltimore City mayor Stephanie Rawlings-Blake, blessed legislation that elevated burning trash to a "tier one renewable energy source" in Maryland's Renewable Energy Portfolio (RPS).[14] An RPS is a type of regulation that requires a jurisdiction, such as a state or county, to gradually transition its energy production from nonrenewable sources such as fossil fuels to renewables like wind and solar. In theory, the RPS incentivized the use of clean, renewable energy, but in practice, according to the Environmental Integrity Project, "WTE [waste-to-energy] incinerators in Maryland typically emit more pollutants per hour of energy produced than Maryland's largest coal-fired power plants."[15] Incineration was dirty energy that relied on the creation of trash when "zero waste" alternatives such as recycling, composting, and "waste recovery" of reusable materials were becoming increasingly available.

The collusion between Maryland's political and economic elite to incentivize burning trash was a matter of public record. The same day the "Waste to Energy Incinerators as Tier One Renewable" bill was signed into law, Energy Answers, the company that would propose the construction of the nation's largest trash-burning incinerator in Curtis Bay, made a $100,000 donation to the Democratic Governors' Associa-

---

and Philip Diamond, "An Environmental History of Fairfield/Wagner Point," https://tinyurl.com/yyxbrptc.

11. A rendering plant processes the "by-products" of animals from slaughterhouses, such as fat, bones, and organs, as well as blood, feathers, and hair.

12. Free Your Voice, "Stop the Incinerator Map," https://tinyurl.com/y287m2t3. While these federal laws regulate what types of and how much toxicity industries are allowed to emit, many plants are not held accountable by state and federal agencies when they do violate these standards.

13. Maryland EHN, "Energy & Health in Maryland," 2–6, https://tinyurl.com/y6mf3vsw.

14. Scott Dance, "How a Trash Incinerator—Baltimore's Biggest Polluter—Became 'Green' Energy," *The Baltimore Sun*, December 15, 2017, https://tinyurl.com/yxd5kyyy.

15. Environmental Integrity Project, "Waste-to-Energy: Dirtying Maryland's Air by Seeking a Quick Fix on Renewable Energy?" https://tinyurl.com/y46k4v35.

tion, which at the time was headed by Governor O'Malley.[16] Labeling burning trash a "tier one renewable" within the Maryland RPS encouraged projects like the proposed Curtis Bay incinerator. It showed little concern for communities that already shouldered a heavy environmental burden by creating the possibility that yet another polluting industry would put down roots in the area.

Within this context in Curtis Bay, students at Benjamin Franklin High School began meeting in the fall of 2012 as a committee of United Workers. United Workers, a human rights organization, was founded in 2002 in an abandoned fire station turned homeless shelter with a commitment to developing and uniting leaders to end poverty. While many might associate human rights with civil and political rights, such as the right to vote, United Workers focuses on the economic and social rights guaranteed by the Universal Declaration of Human Rights, which includes the rights to work, housing, and healthcare.[17] Its first major campaign for a living wage was organized by day laborers working at the iconic Camden Yards baseball stadium. After this initial victory in 2008, United Workers leaders moved on to another city landmark, the Inner Harbor, a downtown tourist district of shops and restaurants. The campaign there resulted in a major settlement in 2013 against the Walt Disney Corporation, the parent company of an ESPN Zone sports bar that closed without adequately warning its workers, in violation of federal law.

With these first victories focused primarily on workers' rights, United Workers began to connect the issues of where people work to where they live, explicitly linking work with dignity to affordable housing and environmental justice. For example, how can a family find affordable housing without a living-wage job to pay the rent? Or how can a home fulfill one's right to housing if it is located in an area with high levels of air pollution that endanger human health? Each of these campaigns, first for work with dignity, and then for housing and a healthy environment, has been fought with a vision toward what United Workers calls "Fair Development."

Fair Development names the vast majority of Baltimore's development as "Failed Development," rejecting the dominant modus operandi when investors attempted to improve the city. United Workers' own analysis pointed out that

16. Annie Linskey, "Firms with Interests in Md. Pour Cash into DGA," *The Baltimore Sun*, November 27, 2011, https://tinyurl.com/yyargkm9.

17. United Nations, "Universal Declaration of Human Rights," https://tinyurl.com/pnjck5h.

during the last 40 years, city and state leaders have looked to economic development as the solution. Significant public resources have been used to transform old industrial areas into tourist sites, featuring restaurants, retail stores, and other forms of hospitality and entertainment. While this development produced some jobs, work in these sectors is low paying, without health insurance and opportunity for upward mobility, and hostile to worker organizing. Because the new housing has been targeted to the well-heeled, real estate values eventually will be pushed beyond the reach of city residents. Environmental burdens (toxins, waste, etc.) of development have fallen disproportionately on communities of color [and the poor].[18]

This failed investment has largely taken place in Baltimore's downtown tourist districts and has produced, as noted above, largely low-wage service-sector jobs. In contrast to the gleaming new shops, restaurants, and office buildings in neighborhoods like Harbor East and Canton in the core of the city, the neighborhoods that need improvement most on the East and West Sides of Baltimore have been ignored for decades through strategic disinvestment. The choice to invest only in certain areas has only deepened the divide between the wealthy and the rest, a divide that in Baltimore also occurs largely along racial lines. Based on the divisions these economic development models have produced over the last several decades, United Workers concluded that the standard models, while they have been profitable for wealthy investors, have not in fact "trickled down" to the communities that need them most and are still struggling to afford basic necessities.

In contrast to development driven largely by the interests of the city's political and economic elite "from above," Fair Development called for the large-scale investment of public resources into community-driven, community-controlled projects "from below." Fair Development projects were focused in the neighborhoods most directly impacted by Failed Development. Fair Development was driven by the principles of universality, equity, transparency, participation, and accountability, as well as the human rights values of respect, dignity, and the sanctity of life.[19] Any development slated to go forward in Baltimore was evaluated in light of these principles and values and underpinned community-based efforts to create work with dignity, permanently affordable housing, and environmental justice. For example, Failed Development projects were typically characterized by a lack of transparency and public participation. The public usually only became aware of projects when they were already largely a "done deal" negotiated behind closed doors

18. United Workers, "Fair Development," https://tinyurl.com/y63zur7e.
19. United Workers, "Principles of Fair Development," https://tinyurl.com/yy889j4o.

without input from the community members who would be directly impacted by the project. By contrast, the Fair Development model emphasized that people directly impacted by a lack of work with dignity, a lack of affordable housing, and environmental injustice must lead so that nothing was done "for the community without the community." Deep processes of community organizing and engagement were needed every step of the way to ensure participation of, and accountability to, the community itself.

Informed by this organizational history and framework, United Workers began working with high school students in Curtis Bay, meeting regularly together to learn about human rights and the principles of Fair Development. Destiny Watford, an emerging leader among the students, narrated that "we created a human rights group called Free Your Voice. As a group we transformed the way we looked at the world in terms of our basic human rights and what we want for ourselves, our families and our communities."[20] The students began to explore what issues were impacting their community and learned that the nation's largest trash-burning incinerator was slated to be built less than a mile away from their school. While plans to build the incinerator had been developing for several years, the students had never heard of it. They learned the incinerator would burn four thousand tons of trash every day and be permitted by law to emit one thousand pounds of lead and 250 pounds of mercury into the air every year, a clear violation of the human rights to clean air and a healthy environment.[21] Lead and mercury are toxic in any amount and have dangerous impacts on human health. Free Your Voice had discovered a clear case of Failed Development in their own community, characterized by a complete lack of transparency and public participation despite the direct impact the incinerator would have on their lives. With this knowledge they began to organize toward a vision of Fair Development in their community.

The students of Free Your Voice were unwilling to accept that an incinerator that would have a direct impact on their health and that of their families would be built less than a mile away from their school. They decided to start knocking on doors in their community to share what they had learned and to find supporters in their struggle to stop the incinerator. Over several months the students were met with a range of reactions, from concern to cynicism. Some residents wanted to hear more, and some closed the door in their faces. Many thought the incinerator was inevitable. After all, Curtis Bay has a long history of being

20. United Workers, "Free Your Voice," https://tinyurl.com/y2h29dl9.
21. Environmental Integrity Project, "Waste-to-Energy" https://tinyurl.com/y46k4v35.

treated as a dumping ground. The incinerator sounded like more of the same kinds of polluting industry that had set up shop in the area for generations. While there was resistance and rejection from many, there was also a growing group of neighbors and supporters willing to join a campaign. By the following summer, Free Your Voice was beginning to develop a campaign narrative, a story they could tell about their efforts as they deepened relationships with their neighbors. In the words of student leader Destiny Watford,

> The pollution threatens our health and our environment. We know the air we breathe isn't clean. . . . However, we lack basic answers to questions about how bad it is. What's worse is that we often don't play a meaningful role in the decisions that affect us. And the only ones who seem to be paying any consequences are community members that have to breathe the air. . . . The last I checked Curtis Bay is a community just like any other. People live here, our children, our families, our friends. I feel the sanctity of human life is not being acknowledged or respected. All of this makes it feel like community members don't matter and aren't relevant, and that we aren't humans at all. But we are. I'm human. All the people of Curtis Bay are humans. As humans we have the right to fair development that respects our rights and puts community needs first. But this will only happen if we begin to learn, reflect, and act together in a way that allows us to solve problems that we're all facing together.[22]

With this initial process of community engagement and a developing story of their struggle, Free Your Voice kept building on its initial momentum, moving from organizing internally to taking its message public.

In December 2013 the Stop the Incinerator campaign led its first major demonstration. Two banners greeted students, teachers, neighbors, and United Workers members from across Baltimore as they gathered on a cold afternoon in the auditorium of Ben Franklin High School. One banner reading "Failed Development" pictured a stack spewing black smoke and the phrase "The Energy Answers incinerator now open for business." In front of the incinerator was a fence with a "No Trespassing" sign. The other banner was titled "Fair Development" and pictured the stack replaced by an enormous tree spreading its branches and leaves. It also showed a young boy and girl walking through thick grass and flowers, the fence less visible on one side. After a brief program of speeches by students and campaign supporters in the auditorium, people gathered outside to march from the school to the site of the proposed incinerator. The Ben Franklin Bayhawks school bus and the students of Free Your

22. United Workers, "Free Your Voice."

Voice led the way, carrying a banner simply stating, "We Demand Fair Development."

The marchers gathered at the proposed site on the side of the road. There was not much to mark the place, just a small white building behind a tall fence, a green sign boasting the "Future Home of Fairfield Renewable Energy," and "No Trespassing" signs. Students and supporters spoke about why they were there and the threat the incinerator posed to the community. After these speeches in the fading light of that winter afternoon, people placed yellow flowers in the fence that glowed in the light of the setting sun, creating a symbol of life and hope where it felt like there was only exclusion and death. This first public demonstration was an important moment of unity for the campaign as students, teachers, and community members came together to stop the incinerator.

A month after the march, Free Your Voice learned that the Baltimore City Public Schools would be purchasing energy from the proposed incinerator through an entity called the Baltimore Regional Purchasing Cooperative. The Purchasing Cooperative included other public school systems and libraries from surrounding counties, as well as the Baltimore Museum of Art and the Baltimore Housing Authority. The students asked how Baltimore City Public Schools could say they were responsible for the safety and well-being of their students if they were purchasing energy from an incinerator that would put their health, and that of the neighborhood in which they lived, at risk.

Free Your Voice decided to take their struggle directly to the Board of the Baltimore City Public Schools. Their goal became to get the Baltimore City Public Schools, as well as other entities within the Regional Purchasing Cooperative, to divest of their contracts with the proposed incinerator. A cancellation of these contracts would reduce the number of customers to which the incinerator could sell its energy, making the incinerator far less economically viable. Free Your Voice tried for several months to get on the agenda of the school board's monthly meetings. Even when a date was finally secured, the group was only allowed two minutes to speak during a public comment period. Although they represented students fighting an issue that directly impacted their community, Free Your Voice was first ignored and then pushed aside. The students became the teachers when they were finally allowed to bring their arguments to the school board.

In their preparations, Free Your Voice worked to create a vivid environment for their presentation. Students, parents, teachers, and campaign supporters brought huge sunflower-shaped banners with the human rights principles of universality, equity, participation, transparency, and accountability emblazoned across them. They also brought another sunflower made from hundreds of smaller sunflower-shaped petitions calling on the Baltimore City School Board and the Baltimore Regional Purchasing Cooperative to opt out of their contracts with the incinerator. (The sunflower became an increasingly important symbol of the Stop the Incinerator campaign because of its historical use in the anti-nuclear movement and its ability to remediate radioactive materials from soil.) Against this backdrop of campaign supporters and artwork, Free Your Voice's presentation included speeches from a student at Vivien T. Thomas High School and a parent from Hamilton Elementary School. It concluded with a spoken word anthem, quoted here in part, from sisters Audrey and Leah Rozier, students of Free Your Voice:

> This life starts with the air that we breathe
> With everyone competitive
> And trying to succeed
> Just worried 'bout the money
> Not the air that we need
> When you think opportunity
> The eye is deceived
> This air quality will help and keep you living
> But with all of this pollution
> It's like good deeds are forbidden
> And everyone is looking to take
> Instead of givin'
> Not knowing that the bad polluted air is all killin'
> The incinerator takes away our breath
> How many do we need
> Until there is nothing that is left
> Until the smoke clogs up and we can't feel our chests
> And the ones who don't catch the symptoms
> Are considered blessed
> The time is now before our planet is destroyed
> Before death is something we cannot avoid
> It's time for change before we don't have a choice
> So let's stand tall together and free our voice
> It'll all get better
> We can save the world
> You gotta free your voice
> From all the boys and the girls.[23]

---

23. Audrey Rozier and Leah Rozier, "Free Your Voice Group Performs in Front of Baltimore City Public Schools Board," https://tinyurl.com/y6ktw6a2.

Every element of Free Your Voice's presentation pointed to the injustices faced by Curtis Bay students and reiterated their call to the school board to divest of its contract with the proposed incinerator. All ten commissioners gave the students a standing ovation, even though they had claimed the meeting for twenty minutes instead of the assigned two. However, only three commissioners accepted an invitation to tour the Curtis Bay community for themselves the following month. This tour was an opportunity to deepen relationships with the school board, for the commissioners to be exposed to the realities of the Curtis Bay community, and for campaign members to continue to press the case for divestment from the incinerator.

Throughout the following fall and winter, the Stop the Incinerator campaign continued to organize gatherings of students, community members, and supporters from across Baltimore City, and Maryland more broadly, to deepen their analysis of the political and economic structures that supported the incinerator and to build unity across a diverse coalition growing to include faith leaders, environmental groups, and artists. I was invited by United Workers, in collaboration with a handful of faith leaders, at this stage in the campaign to help develop a Bible study curriculum that would support Free Your Voice's efforts. The purpose of this curriculum development process, and of the Bible study workshop itself, was to deepen relationships with faith communities in Curtis Bay as well as with faith-rooted environmental groups in Baltimore City and beyond.

READING 1 KINGS 21:1–16 TOGETHER

I met first with a small planning group of organizers connected to the campaign to ground myself in its current dynamics. A number of themes emerged from those conversations, including the importance of a relationship to the land, which was described as "the beating heart of the campaign." Based on these initial conversations I suggested a handful of biblical texts for the workshop. As will be described in chapter 4 (which focuses on facilitation), sometimes the choice of text is collaborative among the organized community and facilitators. Sometimes the facilitators choose the texts in a more directed way, while in other circumstances the community might already have a text in mind. While I directed the selection of the text by narrowing the group's options, the organizers made the ultimate decision for 1 Kings 21:1–16, the story of Naboth's vineyard. After choosing the text, a small planning group of faith leaders, organizers, and facilitators met regularly for several weeks to plan the curriculum. They considered a number of issues, including existing and potential relationships with local faith communities, the level of familiarity participants may or may not already have with the campaign, and how the workshop might be used to invite participants into a deeper relationship with the campaign. The results of that planning process are described below.

The workshop was set to take place in the basement social hall of St. Athanasius, a Roman Catholic church in Curtis Bay. The size of the hall reflected a bygone era when the church had a large, historically white, working class, and mostly Polish-speaking population in the late nineteenth and early twentieth centuries.[24] At the time Curtis Bay was flooded with immigrants working in the nearby factories, participants in the industrial boom described above. These factories were for the most part shuttered, the jobs they once provided, along with the people that worked them, long gone.

The Workshop

The workshop took place on a warm spring morning. When the facilitation team arrived, the parish hall, as expected, was lined by long tables and chairs, one of its walls opened by large windows covered with vertical blinds. The windows framed a view of a sloping hill that met the water of Curtis Bay, a few blocks of houses somewhat obstructing the view of the flecks of sunlight moving across the water. The houses quickly transitioned into the industrial area that lined the bay. In preparation for the participants' arrivals, the facilitation team moved a handful of the banquet tables closest to the windows off to one side and set up metal folding chairs in a circle. The focal point of the space became a small table, simply adorned with a vase of fresh cut sunflowers, sunflowers painted on vinyl from previous actions, an open Bible, a candle, and a cross. A nearby table was covered with a banner from an organization in Puerto Rico also fighting an Energy Answers incinerator.

With the space set, the participants began to arrive—elderly members of St. Athanasius parish, high school students of Free Your Voice, United Workers members from across Baltimore, city residents, and a handful of representatives from faith-rooted environmental justice groups. The parish priest welcomed the participants on behalf of St. Athanasius, and a parishioner offered words of prayer as she lit the candle at the center of the circle. After introductions, Free Your Voice students shared how

24. Community of St. Athanasius and St. Rose of Lima, "History of St. Athanasius," https://tinyurl.com/yxa9j9z8.

they started a campaign to stop an incinerator. They traced the history of their beginnings at Ben Franklin High School, their work in the Curtis Bay neighborhood, and their analysis of what it would take to stop the incinerator's construction. Some parishioners had no idea an incinerator was slated to be built in their neighborhood. The temperature in the room rose somewhat as they expressed righteous indignation, asking why they knew nothing about this project. This deliberate foregrounding of the social location of the neighborhood, and the campaign that emerged in response to it, created a sense of accountability from the outset to the particularities of the Curtis Bay context.

Following introductions to each other and to the campaign, the workshop continued with an introduction of the biblical text. A handout was circulated with a paraphrase of the text and discussion questions. Some participants had brought their own Bibles and some referred to the handout. A handful of participants read 1 Kings 21:1–16 aloud in different voices. The story went like this:

> Naboth of Jezreel has a vineyard beside the palace of Ahab, the king of Samaria. Ahab wants the vineyard for a vegetable garden, offering Naboth a better vineyard or its worth in money for his land. Naboth refuses Ahab, saying, "God forbid me give you the inheritance of my ancestors" (1 Kgs 21:3).[25] Ahab returns to his palace frustrated at Naboth's refusal, laying on his bed with his face turned away, refusing to eat.
>
> Ahab's wife Jezebel asks how he can be so sullen that he eats no food. Ahab tells her about Naboth's refusal. Jezebel chides Ahab, asking if he indeed reigns over Israel. She tells Ahab she will give him Naboth's vineyard.
>
> Jezebel writes letters in Ahab's name, seals them with his seal, and sends them to the elders and nobles in the city, instructing them to proclaim a fast and set two worthless men to testify that Naboth has cursed God and the king. Everyone does as they are told. Naboth is convicted and stoned to death. When Jezebel receives word that Naboth is dead, she tells Ahab to take possession of the vineyard, which he does.

What is this text about?

After the group had heard the story read aloud in different voices, the discussion began with the question "What is this text about?" There was no one "right" answer. Every response was recorded on flipchart paper, both for the practical reason that it allowed the participants access to

---

25. Throughout this chapter both participant responses and the biblical text are placed in quotes. The biblical text is distinguished by the addition of parenthetical citation. Participant responses are transcribed from those recorded on flipchart paper.

each other's responses in a visual as well as an auditory way, and for the methodological reason that it validated the responses of each participant.

This initial question was an effort to suss out from the community gathered what, from the Contextual Bible Study methodology, was "in front of the text." "In front of the text" refers to what received interpretations were already present among the "ordinary readers" in the room. For this group, the story of Naboth's vineyard was largely unfamiliar, and therefore there was not a strong received history of interpretation or preconceived ideas about what the text was about. A prominent response from the participants was that the story was about "land and the possession of it." It was also about the "abuse of power" and "control," as well as specific actions such as "coveting thy neighbor's goods," "not taking *no* for an answer," a "sham trial," "murder to get what you want," "lying," and "deceit." Many of these preliminary responses would develop into themes that informed much of the workshop.

Foregrounded by an introduction to the incinerator campaign and with this initial set of responses to the text read aloud, the study then moved into the second part. These questions were designed to further slow the reading by digging more deeply into its literary dimensions—what, from Contextual Bible Study, is called "on the text." Participants focused on its literary elements that highlighted the text's narrative qualities. These elements included such things as characters, setting, and plot, which were democratically available to all readers regardless of training, in contrast to a text's historical dimensions, which are often not immediately available without further research. The two sets of questions the participants were invited to discuss were:

Who are the characters in this story, and how is each described?

What strategies are used for taking Naboth's vineyard from him?

To encourage a more focused, detail-oriented discussion, in contrast to the broad strokes and initial impressions of the first part, the participants moved from a large group to small groups. There are different ways to facilitate this movement. For this particular study I asked the participants to "count off" into four groups, with the "ones" assigned to one corner of the hall, the "twos" in another, and so forth. At the time I thought heterogeneous groups would allow the participants to "cross-pollinate" among participants who represented different geographies and experiences.[26] After counting off, each group went to work with their own

26. If I were to facilitate this study again with this particular, heterogeneous group, I might divide the participants into affinity groups: the high school students from Free Your Voice, the

set of markers and flipchart, referring to the biblical text in their own Bibles or on the handout. The groups were instructed to choose a scribe to record the group's responses as well as a person who would report out a summary of his/her small group's conversation to the large group. After some shuffling of tables and chairs, a soft buzz filled the hall as the small groups organized themselves. Members of each group read the biblical text aloud again and the discussions continued.

As the facilitator, I circulated around to each small group to answer questions if there were any and/or provide clarification if it was asked for. I did not attempt to insert myself into conversations that were already underway. When the small groups had mostly moved through the questions, I began to transition participants back to where we started in the large group—although certainly not where we started with our initial reading of the text. Instead of attempting to capture the reports of each individual group, in this section I provide summaries of responses from across the groups and point to themes that emerged from them.

"Who are the characters in this story?" "How is each character described?" The participants identified three major characters: Naboth, Ahab, and Jezebel, as well as secondary characters—the elders, nobles, and people of Jezreel, and two "scoundrels" who testified falsely against Naboth. There was not much discussion of the secondary characters by the groups, and I therefore focus here on the three major characters.

Naboth

The groups reported that Naboth is a "Jezreelite" who "owns a vineyard" in Jezreel located next to Ahab's palace (1 Kgs 21:1). They also described Naboth as "respected," "brave," and "God-fearing." These evaluative descriptions were based on a positive identification with his character but did not necessarily have a strong basis in the biblical text itself. I do not make this distinction between a literal reading and the participants' interpretations to imply the participants were "wrong." I only want to point out how quickly responses could move from a literary analysis of

elderly parishioners from St. Athanasius, the staff from environmental and social justice organizations, and the members of United Workers from other parts of Baltimore City each in their own groups. These differences across race, age, geography, educational attainment, and level of political consciousness could, on the one hand, provide for rich discussion through sharing from different experiences or, on the other hand, contribute to certain individuals intentionally or unintentionally dominating the discussion and implicitly silencing the perspectives of others. During this particular study, who took the lead in reporting out each small group's findings (typically organizational staff members who were white and presented as middle class) suggested that certain individuals dominated the small group discussion more than others.

the text itself to creatively engaging a level or two removed from the text.

The biblical text provided no description of Naboth's personality or backstory. From a (post)modern perspective Naboth's character was entirely flat. For example, while his life was at stake, there was no record of Naboth speaking or having an emotional reaction to the trial, although it was possible to imagine any number of feelings he may have been experiencing—rage, betrayal, confusion. There was no account of Naboth defending himself but also no indication he had any opportunity to do so. Naboth's only recorded words were, "God forbid I should give you my ancestral inheritance" (1 Kgs 21:3). The only details the biblical text shared with the reader about Naboth were that he refused to have his land taken away, that he understood the land as his inheritance from God, and that God forbade him to give his land to Ahab.

Related to Naboth's refusal to give up his land, a participant described Naboth as "connected to his ancestral roots." There is debate among biblical scholars as to the exact biblical tradition(s) to which Naboth might be referring in his refusal of Ahab's offer. But the larger point was that Naboth was faithful to a biblical vision of the relationship between God and the land: God distributed and provided the land to God's people, and the land belonged to God.

Ahab

Ahab, in contrast to Naboth, was by no means faithful to God's vision for living in relationship to the land. According to the participants, Ahab was "king of Samaria" (1 Kgs 21:1). He "has a wife." He "wants" Naboth's vineyard. He was variously described as a "brat," "entitled," "greedy," and "having no scruples."

In some ways Ahab seemed reasonable but also weak. He did not simply take Naboth's land. Ahab offered Naboth an even better vineyard or money in exchange for the vineyard next to his palace. On the surface Ahab seemed to be offering Naboth a good deal. Although land was regularly bought and sold in ancient Israel, what was particularly offensive to Naboth was that Ahab wanted to exchange Naboth's inheritance from God.

When Ahab recounted to Jezebel what Naboth said, either his memory was faulty, or he deliberately changed Naboth's words (1 Kgs 21:6). Naboth said to Ahab, "God forbid I should give you my ancestral inheritance" (1 Kgs 21:3). But what Ahab recalled as Naboth's words were, "I will not give you my vineyard" (1 Kgs 21:6). Interestingly Ahab implicitly left God out of the equation. The participants understood Ahab as an almost entirely negative character, although there was room for some complexity and complication in their assessment.

Jezebel

The participants variously described Jezebel as someone who "wrote a letter," "has power," and was an "orchestrator." While Ahab's offer for Naboth's vineyard was the occasion for the story, it was Jezebel's response to Naboth's refusal that moved the story forward. The narrator explained that Ahab came into his house sullen and vexed because of Naboth's refusal (1 Kgs 21:4–5). This moment could easily have been the end of the story—Ahab asked for Naboth's vineyard; Naboth refused; end scene—but it was Jezebel who did not take Naboth's "no" for an answer, saying that she would give Ahab Naboth's vineyard.

Jezebel appealed to Ahab's absolute authority, asking, "Do you not reign over Israel?" The irony was that it appeared it was not Ahab who ruled but Jezebel. Jezebel wrote letters in Ahab's name. She sealed them with his seal. She sent letters to the elders and nobles living with Naboth in his city (1 Kgs 21:8). While Ahab was lying depressed on his couch, Jezebel was getting things done. While Ahab initiated the conflict, it was Jezebel who brought it to conclusion through a series of actions that resulted in false accusations against Naboth, and in his death.

Gender Dynamics

The participants' responses to Jezebel revealed a thread that pointed to what one person described as "the subtle power of women." Some participants perceived a woman who schemes to have an innocent man murdered as the "power behind the man." It was not Ahab but Jezebel who delivered the vineyard over the dead body of Naboth. Ahab appeared weak and Jezebel strong in a reversal of patriarchal gender norms that valued a man acting from a position of authority while a woman passively receives and/or responds to those actions.

The patriarchal values inherent in the biblical text were replicated in some of the participants' responses. While Jezebel was, according to one participant, a "strong" character who "stands up for her husband," there was discomfort among some of the participants about a power to manipulate and control that seemed especially feminine—and was therefore problematic. It was easy, for both the biblical text and the participants, to "blame the woman" for the injustice that had unfolded because it fit squarely within another patriarchal assumption, namely that men were inherently virtuous and women inherently evil. Although not discussed in this particular study, it is important to note that within the broader literary context both Jezebel and Ahab are described as evil. The dichotomy of Ahab as "good," or at the very least a passive victim of Jezebel's scheming, and Jezebel as "evil" does not hold up in the broader literary context.[27] The planning team did not anticipate the emergence of this subtheme around gender dynamics. Indeed, it would have been a Bible study in itself to explore the intersectional issues of gender, power, and different relationships to the land in this story.[28] I include this digression to point to the unanticipated "excesses of meaning" that can emerge. As much as a facilitation team may try to guide a process, biblical texts cannot be easily pinned down or limited to a narrow range of themes.

What strategies are used for taking Naboth's vineyard from him?

With this initial exploration of the main characters, the discussion turned to the specific strategies Ahab, and Jezebel in particular, used to dispossess Naboth of his vineyard. Despite the proclamation of a fast, Naboth had committed no sins in this instance that required repentance (1 Kgs 21:9–10). According to the narrator, Naboth did invoke God and speak with the king, but he cursed neither. However, the text did not suggest there were any witnesses to Naboth and Ahab's conversation. Two "worthless" men claimed Naboth had cursed God and the king. Although there were strong dissonances between what Naboth had actually done and what he was accused of doing, it was Naboth's word

27. Ahab is consistently described as an evil, idolatrous king, the worst of the worst. "Ahab son of Omri did evil in the sight of the Lord more than all who were before him" (1 Kgs 16:30). He actively promotes the worship of Baal, a Canaanite fertility god, in violation of YHWH's commandment that Israel worship no other gods (1 Kgs 16:32–33). Ahab adds insult to injury by marrying a foreign princess, "Jezebel daughter of King Ethbaal of the Sidonians" (1 Kgs 16:31), who is an active collaborator in promoting the idolatrous worship of Baal. In an editorial aside, the biblical text claims, "Indeed, there was no one like Ahab, who sold himself to do what was evil in the sight of the Lord, urged on by his wife Jezebel. He acted most abominably in going after idols, as the Amorites had done, whom the Lord drove out before the Israelites" (1 Kgs 21:25–26).

28. Jezebel also promotes the worship of Baal independent of her husband, by killing prophets of YHWH (1 Kgs 18:4), supporting prophets of Baal and Asherah who eat at her table (1 Kgs 18:19), and threatening to kill Elijah when he kills the prophets of Baal she supported (1 Kgs 19:2). Shoffren notes that because of these actions, Jezebel "is notorious within Tanachic literature for her persecution of the prophets in Israel, and like Ahab inspires the wrath of the redactors." Marc Shoffren, "Educational Approaches to Naboth's Vineyard (1 Kings 21)," *The Journal of Progressive Judaism* 13 (November 1999): 10.

against that of two witnesses. Naboth was condemned to death by stoning (1 Kgs 21:10). One participant suggested a strategy of "murder to get what you want," while another described the trial as a "sham."

The elders, nobles, and witnesses who followed the "king's" orders and conducted the trial were complicit in Naboth's death, although these groups had no real way of knowing truth from fiction. The public story, from the "king" himself, was that Naboth cursed God and his own person. The hidden story, the one only Naboth, Ahab, and Jezebel knew, was that Naboth refused to give up his vineyard for money. Neither Ahab nor Jezebel actually killed Naboth. The "they" who stoned the condemned Naboth is ambiguous. Was it the elders, nobles, people, or some combination of them? Regardless of which group(s) carried out the deed, Naboth was killed by his own people. The issue of complicity continued to be an important theme in the workshop, especially as participants made connections between the biblical story and their own context.

Once each group had an opportunity to report their findings about the story's main characters and strategies, the workshop shifted gears a final time. The third movement joined the biblical text with the group's contemporary context, a return to what was "in front of the text" in light of the literary analysis of the second movement. Although already happening organically throughout the study, this third part was a particular opportunity to make connections between the biblical text and the current situation in Curtis Bay. The next questions the group addressed were what similarities and differences it saw between Naboth's vineyard and the land in Curtis Bay, and between the characters in the story and the incinerator campaign.

What are the similarities and differences between Naboth's vineyard and the land in Curtis Bay? What are the similarities and differences between the characters and the incinerator campaign?

Unsurprisingly, the participants found far more overarching similarities than differences between Naboth's vineyard and Curtis Bay. Several pointed out connections about power and the people that wield it. In both contexts the people were subjected to "power politics." People died as a consequence of decisions the powerful made to maintain their own wealth and status. Naboth's death came as a direct result of stoning by his own people, while in Curtis Bay death was an indirect consequence of air pollution that caused respiratory disease and heart disease. One participant pointed out that in both cases the powerful made the "wrong" decision because they did not protect the rights of the people and the land.

Relatedly, the powerful in both cases appeared to have no qualms about lying. As described above, Jezebel misrepresented herself as the king and told a version of events that did not reflect what the narrator described. In the case of Curtis Bay, Energy Answers lied about the benefits the community would receive, and about the very nature of incineration as a "clean" form of energy. Although not a specific response from the participants, one aspect of power in both contexts was the ability to shape "truth" according to the preferences and worldviews of the powerful.

Several participants spoke to multiple layers of complicity present in the interests of the powerful. Just as the elders and nobles of Jezreel were complicit in Naboth's death, elected officials, from the Baltimore City mayor to the Maryland governor, were complicit in creating the circumstances under which burning trash would be considered a "green" and "renewable" energy. In the case of Naboth's vineyard, "The question is then who is actually guilty of Naboth's death. Those who stone him to death, those who knowingly bear false witness against him, the elders who 'set up' Naboth, Jezebel who instigates the death, or Ahab, who whether knowingly or unknowingly is the cause of the murder and in whose name the act is carried out."[29] It was difficult to point to any one person who was entirely "at fault" for Naboth's death. Similarly, Baltimore City School Board member Cheryl Casciani explained that for the incinerator campaign, "The plant was not breaking any laws, but a community is the sum of its parts. Plant A is putting in so many pounds of mercury, plant B, plant C, plant D. It's a math problem. But each individual plant doesn't have to do the math. So the kids were doing the math."[30] While Energy Answers argued that it could not possibly be directly responsible for the deaths of Curtis Bay residents due to air pollution, the incinerator, regardless of whether it complied with environmental regulations, participated in a system that contributed to a toxic ecosystem in which neither the land, nor the people who live on it, could thrive.

In addition to questions of power and complicity, differing relationships to the land also emerged as a theme in exploring the similarities and differences between Naboth's vineyard and Curtis Bay. In both contexts, what might look like a good development deal in terms of practical and

---

29. Shoffren, "Educational Approaches to Naboth's Vineyard," 9.

30. Starbucks Coffee, "Upstanders—The Kids Who Killed an Incinerator," https://tinyurl.com/yyl9mvun.

beneficial land use in actuality only benefited the powerful. While Ahab suggested Naboth might receive another vineyard or its value in money, ultimately only Ahab and Jezebel profited. Not only was Naboth dispossessed of his land but he lost his life too. Energy Answers touted the incinerator as a source of clean, renewable energy that would improve the Curtis Bay community with promises of jobs and a community benefits agreement. These benefits would supposedly improve the community's relationship to the land. But if it were built, residents would in reality receive no real benefits from the incinerator; rather they faced eventual death both of their own bodies and of the land. While Naboth was given the option to say "no," the right of refusal to sell his land, the people of Curtis Bay were not. The public had no real opportunities to participate or comment before a decision was made to build the incinerator, and there was no way for people to express their opposition to a development deal that would directly impact their health and well-being, as well as that of the land. In both contexts, Naboth and Curtis Bay residents were forced by powerful people to make hard choices about their relationships to the land. The powerful sought to compromise that relationship for their own benefit. With this exploration of these similarities and the nuanced differences between the biblical text and the participants' contemporary context, the workshop concluded with a last question about how to use their insights for the sake of transformation.

What will be our plan of action?

This final question—"What will be our plan of action?"—connected an analysis of the biblical text and the contemporary contexts of the participants with a group response to the workshop. This moment facilitated a process through which the group decided, in light of what it had read and learned, how they would take their collective experience into the world. A Contextual Bible Study process was not done for its own sake but for the purpose of transformation at the service of, and in solidarity with, the struggle of the organized poor. In this particular context, Free Your Voice was in a struggle to stop an incinerator, but the group was also more broadly connected to all the residents of Curtis Bay, to Baltimore City, and to those beyond who would be directly impacted by the air pollution the incinerator would create. In order to be accountable to this particular context, members of the incinerator campaign shared ways in which the participants could connect with this struggle.

In the same way that the initial readings of the text were prefaced by an introduction to the incinerator campaign, before the large group addressed this final question, participants shared several ways to connect with the campaign. A community resident explained a plan she had engineered to turn the incinerator site into a solar field. A representative of a local faith-rooted environmental group provided ways in which local churches audited their energy use and implemented more environmentally sustainable practices. A member of Free Your Voice outlined upcoming campaign events. While these examples might seem directed, the planning team's intent was to make the workshop as accessible as possible. It made no assumption that the participants would be familiar with possible modes of community engagement.

In response to these initial suggestions, the participants offered several of their own, including a peaceful picket at City Hall to raise public awareness about the incinerator. Another idea was for the participants to share what they had learned with St. Rose of Lima, St. Athanasius's sister parish. In general, participants wanted to do more to educate one another in the local community through word of mouth and the media. A common theme throughout this part of the discussion was the particular role churches had to play in speaking from a place of moral authority. With these action steps in place, the study concluded with a closing prayer. With the formal conclusion of the workshop, some participants lingered for several minutes of continued conversation and reflection before filtering out of the parish hall.

What Happened Next

Within a month after the Bible study workshop described above, two major campaign events unfolded. The first was United Workers and Free Your Voice organizing a Fair Development concert that brought together hundreds of community members and campaign supporters to celebrate the arts and culture emerging from the campaign. The second was that the Baltimore Regional Purchasing Cooperative, which included Baltimore City Public Schools, opted out of its contract with the Energy Answers incinerator. It was only through continuous public pressure and grassroots organizing that the Purchasing Cooperative finally made this decision. Disinvestment from this major contract was an important intermediate victory that made the incinerator far less economically viable, but it not end Energy Answers' attempts to construct.

Around this point in the campaign Free Your Voice learned that Energy Answers was in violation of its building permits, and not for the first time. For example, in June 2014 Energy Answers was ordered to stop construction because it had failed to buy energy offsets, which were basically the right to pollute.[31] In 2016, Energy Answers had not constructed on the site of the proposed incinerator in over eighteen months. In theory, the incinerator would not be able to legally construct if the Maryland Department of Energy (MDE) withdrew Energy Answers' building permits. In practice it would take tremendous public pressure to move the MDE to respond to the most conservative of demands, to enforce the law by actually withdrawing the permits. While there was clear evidence, even by the admission of the MDE itself, that Energy Answers was in violation of its permits and therefore was not legally allowed to construct, the MDE had limited political will to actually enforce the law by withdrawing the permits. Without Free Your Voice's research and ongoing public pressure from campaign supporters, the MDE most likely would have continued the status quo of allowing Energy Answers to construct, despite the fact that it was breaking the law in doing so.

The next phase of the campaign began in summer 2016 with the simple demand to the MDE to enforce the law by withdrawing Energy Answers' expired building permits. This demand was met with silence for months, despite the hundreds of letters, petitions, and phone calls made to the MDE offices. Free Your Voice redelivered the demand letter to pull the permits that November with the imposition of a month-long deadline for a response. That deadline came with the promise that if their demand continued to be ignored, the letter would be redelivered yet again by members of the public.

The MDE did not publicly respond by the December deadline to enforce the law and pull Energy Answers' permits. In response, on the appointed day, hundreds of campaign supporters gathered outside the MDE offices in Baltimore City, which are located inside a large, privately owned office building. MDE officials clearly had received the redelivered demand letter because locked gates and security guards greeted the gathering crowd. While these members of the public simply wanted to redeliver their demands, exercising their democratic right to petition a government office, they were denied entry. A long negotiation ensued between the MDE officials who arrived outside the gates to the office complex and campaign leaders. Only nine people of the hundreds present were allowed entry to redeliver petitions on behalf of the gathered. Once they were escorted to the MDE offices, a long conversation began between MDE secretary Ben Grumbles, his advisors, and

31. Scott Dance, "Construction of Fairfield Power Plant Ordered Halted over Air Quality Permit Violation," *The Baltimore Sun*, June 24, 2014, https://tinyurl.com/y332xy9n.

the delegation, which reiterated their demand, yet again, that the Energy Answers permits be pulled.

When it became clear that the MDE had no intention of responding to this demand one way or the other, the majority of the delegation refused to leave until the permits were pulled and the law enforced. Despite the fact that the conversation had ended in a non-resolution, it took the MDE officials present several minutes to respond to the fact that the delegation was not leaving. They called the building manager, who in turn called the police. The police arrested seven volunteers from the delegation, including me. We had been training for months, knowing there was a very real possibility the action might unfold in this way. Both inside the MDE offices and outside the gates of the office complex, the police made an overwhelming display of force through the presence of dozens of officers and vehicles, including officers dressed in riot gear, although both the crowds gathered and the arrestees themselves remained nonviolent throughout the evening. Although the arrests of the "Incinerator Seven" continued to draw attention and media coverage to the issue, it was not until March of the following year that the MDE finally decided to pull the Energy Answers permits. This decision effectively ended the company's ability to legally construct and forestalled any economic viability of the incinerator project. It was a huge victory for Free Your Voice and the residents of Curtis Bay who stopped an incinerator and protected their community's rights to clean air and a healthy environment.

Just a month later in April 2016, Destiny Watford, one among many of the student leaders of Free Your Voice, was awarded the Goldman Environmental Prize for North America in acknowledgment of the work of dozens of student leaders, as well as hundreds of community members and campaign supporters. The Goldman Prize is widely regarded as the highest recognition of grassroots environmental leaders in the world. It "recognizes individuals for sustained and significant efforts to protect and enhance the natural environment, often at great personal risk."[32] In her acceptance speech Watford stated,

> The fact that burning trash is legal in my state and considered a renewable energy source tied to receiving public subsidies for climate solutions like wind and solar is a clear sign that our system is failing us and our planet. This is why we have to take the lead. Those directly impacted by the injustices we face know firsthand that this is a matter of survival, and that there is a need for a new vision that is based on our basic human rights, environ-

32. The Goldman Environmental Prize, "About the Prize," https://tinyurl.com/y5sd2ps4.

mental justice, and the belief that all life is sacred. We decided that it isn't the fate of our community or our planet to be treated as a dumping ground.

In her speech Destiny Watford called on the FMC Corporation to liberate the ninety acres of land Energy Answers had leased to construct the incinerator for community-driven development projects, such as a solar farm. As with Naboth's vineyard, the life and death of Curtis Bay is bound up in its relationship to the land.

While Free Your Voice and its supporters defeated an incinerator, the struggle is by no means over. Curtis Bay is still a neighborhood faced by significant poverty, and it is surrounded by industries that pollute the air, water, and land on a daily basis. Since its first major victory, the incinerator campaign has turned to a focus on the development of a "zero waste" plan for Baltimore City, on the exploration of truly green, community-controlled energy alternatives such as solar cooperatives, and on connecting the issue of land to a lack of affordable housing. The struggle for justice for the land, and human rights for the people who live on it, is not over. In a lot of ways, it is only just beginning with the leaders who have been forged and united through this struggle.

3.

An Empty Tomb and Empty Homes: Mark 16:1–8

On the East and West Sides, as well as in neighborhoods across Baltimore, entire blocks of rowhomes stood abandoned in various states of disrepair. Windows were boarded up with plywood, which quickly turned gray from exposure to the elements. Collapsed roofs caved in to second and then first floors, sometimes falling all the way to the basement. Wooden braces extending onto sidewalks propped up brick facades that threatened to crumble. Sometimes houses were so structurally unsound they did fall down. In March 2016 a man sitting in his Cadillac outside a rowhome was killed when the building collapsed, crushing him in his car.[1] On the doors of many houses was a red square with a white "X." This sign warned that the building was unsafe, condemned, and unfit for human habitation. A colloquial term for these abandoned houses was "the vacants." The most visible symptom of Baltimore's housing crisis, these vacants created in some parts of the city the impression of a gutted, post-industrial wasteland.

I share these images not to suggest Baltimore is in any way unique, somehow different than the realities many US Americans face, although perhaps in some places they are less visible. Baltimore was and is similar to post-industrial cities across the United States, such as Pittsburgh and Detroit. The relative prosperity of the industrial era created a need to house workers and their families. In the 1970s and 1980s, manufacturing largely began to move to cheaper labor markets and/or to mechanize.

1. Tim Prudente, "Collapse: The Rise and Deadly Fall of a Baltimore Rowhouse," *The Baltimore Sun*, July 12, 2018, https://tinyurl.com/y3a5fnvz.

Now robots are increasingly doing the work human beings once did.[2] With the manufacturing jobs that provided family-sustaining wages for much of the city's population largely gone, Baltimore's population has been steadily declining for decades. The rowhomes that stand vacant today are a part of that bygone era.[3] This historic shift from manufacturing to a post-industrial, digital economy has reshaped Baltimore.

In the wake of deindustrialization, the jobs that have been created were largely in the service sector, in industries such as retail, entertainment, and hospitality. These jobs were low-paying, had irregular work schedules, and avoided providing benefits often by offering less than full-time hours.[4] The insecurity created by a lack of family-sustaining jobs was compounded with the criminalization of black and brown peoples through racist overpolicing of certain neighborhoods.[5] When people were released and sought employment, it was difficult to find employers willing to hire people with criminal records, leading to high unemployment rates among people who were formerly incarcerated.[6] During the post–World War II industrial period of relative prosperity, larger sections of the population were able to meet their basic needs, but the post-industrial shift toward low-wage jobs in the service sector has made it

2. The ways in which automation is reshaping the nature of work are a matter of intense debate. For one perspective, Willie Baptist, a lifelong organizer and scholar, writes, "Because of how [digital and automating] technology has been utilized in the capitalist process, i.e., to eliminate labor, we have, in fact, come to a point where the production system has become 'too productive.' Increased productivity and increased joblessness is thereby producing declining 'final demand' for surplus goods and services. This is forcing capital to move out of the 'real economy' to the speculative economy in search of profits." Willie Baptist, *It's Not Enough to Be Angry* (New York: University of the Poor Press, 2015), chap. 5.

3. Marilyn Kindrick Julius and Luis Larín, "Baltimore Economic Reality Tour," paper presented at the Annual Meeting of the Society of Biblical Literature, Baltimore, Maryland, November 22, 2013, 3–4.

4. For extensive documentation of the trends toward temporizing and casualizing jobs in the service sector in Baltimore's downtown tourist district, see United Workers and The National Economic and Social Rights Initiative, "Hidden in Plain Sight: Workers at Baltimore Inner Harbor and the Struggle for Fair Development," https://tinyurl.com/y2mxdze4.

5. On August 10, 2016, a US Department of Justice investigation found, in the wake of the murder of Freddie Gray, that the Baltimore police department "engages in a pattern or practice of conduct that violates the Constitution and federal law, including: (1) making unconstitutional Stops, Searches, and Arrests; (2) using enforcement strategies that produce severe and unjustified disparities in the rates of Stops, Searches, and Arrests of African Americans; (3) using excessive force; and (4) retaliating against people engaging in constitutionally-protected expression." United States District Court for the District of Maryland, "United States of America, Plaintiff v. Police Department of Baltimore City, et. al., Defendants," https://tinyurl.com/y4gvyntys.

6. According to the Prison Policy Initiative, "formerly incarcerated people are unemployed at a rate of over 27%—higher than the total U.S. unemployment rate during any historical period, including the Great Depression." These findings are supported by this longitudinal study: S. K. S. Shannon, C. Uggen, J. Schnittker et al., "The Growth, Scope, and Spatial Distribution of People with Felony Records in the United States, 1948–2010," *Demography* 54 (2017): 1795.

increasingly difficult for families to make ends meet, including finding permanently affordable housing.

The current housing crisis in Baltimore is the product of a long history of racist and discriminatory housing policy on the part of the county's economic and political institutions. In the early nineteenth century, zoning was used to restrict black families to only a few neighborhoods. Then racially restrictive covenants were placed in housing deeds, preventing whites from selling their homes to black families.[7] At the same time, banks and the Federal Housing Authority only made mortgage insurance available to white families in specific neighborhoods. Through a practice called "redlining," banks and the federal government created maps that literally drew red lines around neighborhoods to which they would not provide service.[8] This strategic disinvestment in city neighborhoods and the incentivization of home ownership after World War II caused whites to flee to the suburbs.[9] These interconnected practices contributed to the depopulation of many neighborhoods, and for people who did stay, or moved in, an increasing lack of basic services like transportation and quality education and healthcare.

This history of deindustrialization and discriminatory policies has created a housing situation in Baltimore characterized by abandonment and absentee landlordism on the one hand, and speculation and gentrification on the other. As white families fled to the suburbs, certain neighborhoods became "blighted," run down through a lack of investment. In these neighborhoods, landlords perceived no incentive to invest in redeveloping their properties and, in the majority of cases, have little connection to the neighborhood.[10] Instead absentee landlords allowed their properties to fall into disrepair, charging rent for often insect- and rodent-infested houses, but maintained ownership as a speculative investment in the hopes that the property would be worth more in the future.

In some neighborhoods, private, for-profit real estate developers bought up these run-down properties at low rates and invested money in fixing them up, adding significantly to their value. When developers remodeled the homes, the current tenants were then asked to leave

---

7. Baltimore Housing Roundtable, "Community Land Trust: Tools for Development without Displacement," 9, https://tinyurl.com/y3y6wee3.

8. Baltimore Housing Roundtable, "Community Land Trust."

9. Antero Pietila, *Not in My Neighborhood: How Bigotry Shaped a Great American City* (Chicago: Ivan R. Dee, 2010), 211–21.

10. A survey of one neighborhood on the East Side organized by Housing Our Neighbors indicated that the overwhelming majority of properties were owned by individuals, as well as public and private entities, outside the neighborhood and frequently outside the city. Baltimore Housing Roundtable, "Community Land Trust," 22.

temporarily during construction. But when the redevelopment was finished, the new rental rates were often double or even triple what the tenants were paying. They could no longer afford to live in their homes, and the new developer displaced them, forcing people to seek more affordable housing in other parts of the city or outside the city.[11] This process, known as gentrification, was a type of redevelopment that displaced low-income residents to make way for middle- and upper-class residents.

As a result of these factors Baltimore was one of the most expensive rental housing markets in the country relative to the income of its population.[12] Housing was considered unaffordable when a family spends more than a third of its income on its cost. In Baltimore one in three "city households are at risk of homelessness or are without housing"[13] because of the cost of housing relative to household income. It was often less expensive to own a home than to rent, but many low-income people were trapped by renting at higher rates because they could not afford to save the money required for a down payment on a mortgage. Ironically, poverty was expensive. For many, housing had simply become unaffordable.

For many in Baltimore, having a roof over one's head was simply too expensive, and the housing situation was one full of contradictions. There was still abundance in the midst of tremendous abandonment. According to official Baltimore City estimates, in 2017 approximately 2,700 people experienced homelessness on any given night,[14] and yet there were approximately sixteen thousand vacant houses.[15] The issue, then, was not a lack of housing but that the people who needed it most were unable to afford it. Baltimore was not so different from the rest of

---

11. A recent example of housing displacement from Baltimore is the "Chapel NDP Apartments, a HUD-subsidized development of 173 affordable townhomes, formerly located in Washington Hill near the Johns Hopkins Hospital. As part of the planned gentrification of the Hopkins area with the intent of capitalizing on the hospital's expansion, Chapel NDP was sold to private developers who demolished all of the townhomes in 2005 with the city's blessing and without a right of return for Chapel NDP residents. A 304-unit luxury apartment complex known as Jefferson Square Apartments arose in its place in 2014. Rent for a two-bedroom unit at Jefferson Square starts at $2,665 per month." Baltimore Housing Roundtable, "Community Land Trust," 18.

12. Philip M. E. Garboden, "The Double Crisis: A Statistical Report on Rental Housing Costs and Affordability in Baltimore City, 2000–2013," *The Abell Report* 29, no. 1 (May 2016), https://tinyurl.com/y3uuqhwv.

13. Baltimore Housing Roundtable, "Community Land Trust," 2.

14. Baltimore Mayor's Office of Human Services, "Baltimore Point in Time Count: January 22, 2017: Preliminary Report," https://tinyurl.com/y6jzpyqa.

15. Housing Authority of Baltimore City, "Baltimore Housing Frequently Asked Questions," https://tinyurl.com/y377vokd.

the country in that, in addition to the poverty experienced by the majority, there was a minority that experienced relative wealth and prosperity.

These contradictions expressed themselves not just along class lines but also along intersecting racial lines. In Baltimore this divide expressed itself geographically through what has been described as the "black butterfly and the white L." The majority of people of color, including African Americans and Latinx, lived in poverty concentrated in the outer parts of the city with a minority of whites living in the center in relative wealth.[16] The disparities between people of color and whites in Baltimore were stark.

> Median household income for African-Americans in Baltimore is nearly half that of whites, $33,801 compared to $62,751. . . . More than two-thirds of black residents of Baltimore don't have enough liquid savings to survive for three months in case of job loss, compared to less than a third of whites. And the unemployment rate for black households in Baltimore is more than three times the rate for white households.[17]

The divides between these different parts of the city reflected structural inequality through differentiated access to, and investment in, basic services such as transportation, healthcare, housing, and education.[18] Just as there was enough housing for all the people without homes in Baltimore, there was also enough wealth to ensure equity between people of color and whites. Amid this mix of poverty and wealth, abandonment and abundance, United Workers developed and united leaders to address these contradictions.

HISTORY OF THE HOUSING IS A
HUMAN RIGHT CAMPAIGN

United Workers is a human rights organization led by low-wage workers based in Baltimore. Founded in 2002, the organization began with campaigns in specific workplaces, first at the iconic Camden Yards baseball stadium and then the Inner Harbor. Both sites attracted thousands of tourists to the city every year and at the same time exploited thousands of workers at poverty wages in difficult working conditions. The real victory that came out of these initial struggles—in addition to

16. Lawrence Brown, "Two Baltimores: The White L vs. the Black Butterfly," *City Paper*, June 28, 2016, https://tinyurl.com/yyw4ke4u.

17. Carrie Wells, "Report Highlights Economic Disparities between Races in Baltimore," *The Baltimore Sun*, January 30, 2017, https://tinyurl.com/y6663zcm.

18. Brown, "Two Baltimores."

tangible wins for a living wage for the stadium workers at Camden Yards and a settlement from the Walt Disney Company for the workers of the ESPN Zone restaurant—was the development of leaders who emerged from these struggles committed to ongoing work for justice and human rights.

With these initial campaigns, United Workers started making connections between where people work and the communities in which they live. In addition to the exploitative conditions that people faced on the job, they also faced struggles around housing, healthcare, education, and the environment. It was out of this context that the Housing Is a Human Right campaign first developed within the broader campaign for Fair Development described in the previous chapter. It sought to address the contradiction described above between the thousands of people in Baltimore who were homeless on any given night and the thousands of houses that stood vacant but ready to offer shelter to human beings. Leaders quickly identified that the lack of affordable housing was not an issue of scarcity. An abundance of empty housing stock existed in Baltimore. The issue was one of distribution in a market-based system that valued profit over people and increasingly pushed housing prices toward unaffordability.

One of the ways that inequality in Baltimore could be addressed was through ensuring that all people, regardless of what race and in which neighborhood they were born, had a home that was permanently affordable. Housing was currently treated as a commodity, as something to be bought and sold on the market. One approach to addressing these issues of inequality was to treat housing instead as a public good, meaning that it was no different than a fire station or a library. It was a service provided by the state for the public good of all because it is necessary for human flourishing.

During the summer of 2013, Housing Our Neighbors (HON), a community group led by people without homes fighting for the human right to housing,[19] surveyed vacant houses on the East Side of Baltimore to better understand the extent of the crisis as well as to identify Fair Development supporters in areas directly impacted by the vacants. The results were striking. For every ten vacant houses volunteers identified, city records only recognized six. The implication was that if city records were undercounting vacant houses by at least 40 percent, the extent of the housing crisis was far deeper than official statistics indicated.[20] HON also learned that the vast majority of vacants identified were owned by

---

19. Housing Our Neighbors, "About Us," https://tinyurl.com/yxfr9xyl.
20. Baltimore Housing Roundtable, "Community Land Trust," 2.

people living outside the neighborhood. Only 3 percent were owned by neighborhood residents.[21] Baltimore City, nearby Johns Hopkins University, and private investors were buying and selling most of the properties. The last three sales of each identified vacant totaled nearly $30 million.[22] Despite this large sum of money circulating to the benefit of these public and private entities, the neighborhood itself had seen no investment.

To point out these contradictions, to celebrate the completion of the survey, and to build further momentum for the Housing Is a Human Right campaign, Housing Our Neighbors, United Workers, and the Baltimore Housing Roundtable organized an "art takeover" in December 2015. For weeks, campaign supporters created artwork on plywood that would cover boarded-up homes on a block in the same neighborhood where the survey was conducted. On the morning of the takeover, the art was nailed over the decaying boards already on the vacants. One was painted like a black chalkboard with the words "This house could be . . ." As supporters gathered, they wrote their visions for the house, the ways in which it could be transformed to serve the community as a clinic, a senior center, a recreation center for children, a barber shop, or even a base for organizing people who were homeless. The art served as backdrop for a press conference as community and faith leaders shared their experiences conducting the survey and the impact the housing crisis was having on the neighborhood, and they called for the need for a change.

That same summer of 2013 that Housing Our Neighbors began surveying vacants on the East Side of Baltimore, United Workers started convening the Baltimore Housing Roundtable. The Roundtable included people directly impacted by an inability to find affordable housing, everyday Baltimore residents, and policy advocates. The intention for this space was to gather a broad diversity of people—renters, home owners, and people without homes to study and find solutions for the housing crisis in Baltimore. A goal was to discuss "links between vacant housing, homelessness, and public policy"[23] and to create a base from which to launch a future campaign to address the crisis in Baltimore City.

The Roundtable intentionally brought together community-based and nonprofit organizations working from a variety of perspectives.

21. Baltimore Housing Roundtable, "Community Land Trust," 2.

22. Baltimore Housing Roundtable, "Community Land Trust," 2.

23. Peter Sabonis, "Baltimore Housing Roundtable: Building a Movement for Permanently Affordable Housing and Community Driven Development," presentation given at National Economic and Social Rights Initiative Meeting, New York, October 2017.

Organizations working on different aspects of an issue like housing are often forced to compete with one another for funding from government entities and foundations, as well as for members and supporters. As separate entities, organizations are typically limited in the types of change they are able to bring about, often providing direct services with little focus on making structural changes through new laws and public policy.[24] From its inception, the Roundtable's vision was to bring together individuals and organizations from a diversity of experiences and perspectives to preempt the kind of "divide and conquer" dynamics they were often up against.

As a result of ongoing study and discussion, by the fall of 2013 the Baltimore Housing Roundtable identified community land trusts (CLTs) as a key tool for creating community-owned, community-controlled, permanently affordable housing in Baltimore City. Community land trusts were "a hybrid between public and private housing, as well as private and community property ownership. CLTs utilize a unique 'ground lease' structure, which affords individuals and families ownership of the home while the CLT retains ownership of the land."[25] Community land trusts have been created across the United States, including in urban housing markets similar to Baltimore City's. To date there are more than 250 community land trusts across the country in every region from the Deep South to the Midwest, New England to the Pacific Northwest.[26] As of 2013, there were already three community land trusts in Baltimore City itself, one of which—the Charm City Land Trust—had been working to preserve green spaces for over a decade and two in the process of acquiring their first properties: the North East Housing Initiative and

24. For the ways in which nonprofit organizations are often forced to compete against one another and participate in the "nonprofit industrial complex"—a web of state, non-profit, and corporate actors that often serve to preempt and co-opt social movements—see INCITE!, *The Revolution Will Not Be Funded: Beyond the Non-Profit Industrial Complex* (Durham: Duke University Press, 2017).

25. Baltimore Housing Roundtable, "Community Land Trust," 24. Part of what makes community land trusts effective is that they create housing that is permanently affordable. The owner of a community land trust home covenants with the trust that, when it comes time to sell, the owner will do so at an affordable price to another low-income buyer. Often what is initially created as low-income housing will convert to market-based housing after the original owner sells. What distinguishes community land trusts from other types of development is that permanent affordability is built into its structure. There is a refusal to participate in a market-based system of buying and selling focused exclusively on making a profit from a basic human right like housing.

26. "Overview: Community Land Trusts (CLTs)," Community-Wealthy.org, https://tinyurl.com/y5lu4jyp; Baltimore Housing Roundtable, "Community Land Trusts 101," 18, https://tinyurl.com/y6oxdwff.

the Greater Baybrook Community Land Trust.[27] What made this type of development community-owned was that the land was held in trust, collectively owned, while the individual family bought the home on the land, made regular mortgage payments like any other home owner, and leased the land on which the home was built from the trust.

What made community land trusts community-controlled was that land trusts were governed by residents themselves alongside residents from the surrounding neighborhoods and policy advocates. The vast majority of development in Baltimore had been driven by decisions made behind closed doors by government officials and private, for-profit developers, with little or no input from the communities that would be impacted by that development. The board of directors of a community land trust is based on a shared-governance model in which homeowners, community members, and members of the broader public, such as public officials and/or housing experts, each have an equal say and vote in the decision-making processes.

Working with the goal of supporting and creating community land trusts to address the lack of affordable housing in the city, the Baltimore Housing Roundtable continued to evolve as a coalition of organizations. In addition to being a gathering place for discussion and study, the Roundtable began to take on a coordinating role among individuals and organizations for policy advocacy, city-wide community organizing, technical assistance for established and newly forming land trusts, and the creation of independent grassroots media.[28]

Working alongside the Roundtable, United Workers continued organizing residents on the East and West Sides of Baltimore. One of the processes through which this work took place was "speak out" events. During these gatherings, leaders shared how housing impacted their daily lives. In the face of a US American culture that valued individualism, pulling oneself up by one's bootstraps, and personal success, shame could often prevent people from sharing their struggles. Instead, people internalized individual and family hardship as a form of personal failure. Countering these deeply embedded cultural tendencies, speak-out events built community and began to break the isolation many felt. They worked to shift people's thinking and perceptions. A lack of affordable housing in Baltimore was not the result of "personal problems" or the moral failings of individuals but rather of a system that failed to treat housing as a public good and a human right.

Some of the themes that emerged from these dialogues were problems

27. Baltimore Housing Roundtable, "Community Land Trusts in Baltimore," https://tinyurl.com/y5uv3kgw.
28. Sabonis, "Baltimore Housing Roundtable."

caused by the vacants and a lack of affordable housing in the city. During a speak-out on the East Side, Shantress Wise, a member of the United Workers leadership council, shared the following:

> I've had to move sixteen times and face countless examples of our broken housing system. My first experience was dealing with a developer back in 2009. I was living in the West Baltimore area, the Penn North area. A developer came to my block and bought up the whole block and started pushing us out of our homes. He only gave us sixty days of notice. They promised us that we could come back into the homes after they finished rehabbing the homes. But that was a broken promise. They raised the rent double time what we were paying and we never came back into that neighborhood. My second experience was in 2010 when I lost my home. I was a housekeeper and I took off for surgery. When I took off for surgery my job paid me all my time . . . and when I came back within two weeks I was no longer on the schedule. I had been there ten years working as a housekeeper. So that's the first time in my life that I started facing to be homeless. . . . I couldn't get help from anyone. I even resorted to sleeping in an emergency room of a hospital. I ended in the Curtis Home shelter for women and kids and went to assisted living from there and then into transitional housing.[29]

Unfortunately, Wise's story was by no means unique; it was shared alongside dozens of others during the speak-outs. When leaders began to see how their isolated experiences were connected, they could envision working together in Baltimore.

Alongside these public events, Roundtable leaders identified the need to articulate for themselves solutions to the affordable housing crisis in Baltimore. As part of its commitment to leadership development and political education, United Workers organized its first leadership school focused on housing in the fall and early winter of 2014. For twelve weeks, leaders met to study the political and economic causes of the housing crisis, share and reflect on their own experiences, and develop skills for developing other leaders. Combined with the work of the Baltimore Housing Roundtable as a whole, leadership development was an important component of building specific community land trusts.

Within this organizational history specifically and in the context of the housing crisis in Baltimore more broadly, I was invited to help develop a Bible study curriculum to deepen relationships among local churches interested in housing issues with United Workers. At the time, I was working with the Poverty Initiative, a partner organization of United Workers. The Poverty Initiative has since been renamed the Kairos Cen-

---

29. United Workers, "Shantress Wise Testimony: East Side Speakout for Fair Development," https://tinyurl.com/y62vthf5.

ter for Religions, Rights, and Social Justice. United Workers organizers said something like, "We're a bunch of lefty organizers. We don't really know how to talk with churches. But we do know about group study as a form of leadership development. We think Bible studies might be an interesting way to do that." Out of that invitation evolved the process described in the next section.

The workshop described below grew out of three years of partnership among three Catholic parishes in North East Baltimore, United Workers, the Baltimore Housing Roundtable, and the North East Housing Initiative.[30] The parishioners began meeting with United Workers with a specific interest in the Housing Is a Human Right campaign and over several months explored what collaboration might look like. Several parishioners had experience working on housing issues as well as other aspects of social justice. Out of this growing partnership parishioners identified a need to understand more deeply human rights values and Fair Development principles. The committee proposed Bible study as a way to deepen that understanding. A small working group developed an initial Bible study series for the 2012 Lenten season. From those first steps, a three-year cycle of lectionary-based studies developed in the liturgical seasons of Advent, Christmas, and Lent. Each study had its own character, with a different format and theme. Each typically formed as a multi-part series, meeting for a few evening hours each week for four to five weeks. Some integrated the writings of human rights leaders such as Rev. Dr. Martin Luther King Jr. and Archbishop Oscar Romero. These processes were foundational for the workshop described below, which evolved out of those experiences and the lessons learned from them. Challenges that emerged from these series are described in more detail in chapter 4.

GATHERING AROUND MARK 16:1–8

The planning process for the Lenten retreat itself became a place for theological and textual reflection as the curriculum developed. For example, Father Ty Hullinger pointed out that in Mark 16:1–8 the first reaction to the first "proof" of the resurrection was surprise, shock, and terror. He hoped the study would create a space in which people could identify on some level with what the women experienced, and that the participants

---

30. The descriptions of these processes are from my own notes, email exchanges among the planning and facilitation teams of various workshops, and the responses to the Bible study workshops and facilitation trainings. Participant responses during workshops are set in quotation marks.

would not immediately jump to solutions but try to sit with the emptiness. He said the shock the women at the tomb experienced was not so
different from trauma people experienced in relationship to the housing crisis in Baltimore. To help sit with this tension, the group decided
to schedule the retreat for the Saturday before the start of Holy Week,
still within the season of Lent, yet anticipating the events of the week to
come in which the passion, crucifixion, and resurrection of Jesus would
be remembered.

During the planning process, the "foreclosure X" emerged as a central
symbol, both in terms of the emptiness it represented and its similarity
to the cross. The foreclosure X was a sign everywhere on the East and
West Sides of Baltimore, posted on row after row of empty, abandoned
houses. It was a warning sign that these houses were condemned and
not fit for human habitation. Father Ty wrote in an email, "The image
of the red and white signs on Baltimore's condemned row homes is,
for me, a ubiquitous symbol of emptiness: empty homes, empty lives,
empty streets, empty neighborhoods and empty policies, empty plans,
and empty promises by our City government and business development
leaders."[31] The group connected the emptiness of condemned houses
represented by the foreclosure X to the emptiness of the tomb. Both
were seen as sites of (potential) resurrection, where witnessing the movement from death to life could take place.

The planning group saw the foreclosure X not only as a symbol of
emptiness but also as a St. Andrew's cross. Both the cross in Mark's
Gospel and the foreclosure X in Baltimore were signs of a particular type
of condemnation and death. Jesus was condemned to die and nailed to
a cross. Under the Roman Empire, crucifixion was a particularly painful
and gruesome form of execution reserved for the lowest of the low in
Roman society, seditious rebels and slaves. In Baltimore, houses were
condemned to vacancy and crosses were nailed on their boarded-up
doors and windows. The cross pointed to a similar social and ideological position in both Jesus's crucifixion and Baltimore's vacants. Father Ty
wrote that the foreclosure X which could be seen "as a warning sign that
'this empty space is dangerous' also speaks to me about the dangerous-
ness of challenging the status quo and ourselves with a gospel text that
calls us to examine carefully the emptiness of today as a catalyst of change
for tomorrow."[32] Perhaps the vacants and the people who once occupied them in Baltimore had experienced their own type of crucifixion at
the margins of society. These symbols of emptiness and the cross were

31. Ty Hullinger, email correspondence, February 17, 2015.
32. Ty Hullinger, email correspondence, February 17, 2015.

important threads that ran through the planning process for the Lenten retreat, informing the curriculum that would ultimately be developed for the day. Rooted in the lessons learned from previous Bible studies and informed by the textual and theological reflections of the planning group, the preparations undertaken for the Lenten retreat gave way to the day itself.

The place the planning group chose for the Lenten retreat was called the "Sunday Room" of St. John's United Methodist Church in the Charles Village neighborhood. The original sanctuary had long since been converted into a multi-purpose community space run by a cooperative used for a range of community events from concerts to film screenings and wedding receptions. What was now the sanctuary of St. John's, the Sunday Room, had previously been the social hall behind the original sanctuary.

The focal wall of the Sunday Room was exposed brick. On it hung a large wooden cross and a series of long, narrow, handmade banners. A simple wooden podium served as a lectern, and a rack of name tags with ribbons greeted people at the door. To the left a rainbow pride flag hung from a balcony. A brown paper mural of construction-paper fish swimming through white bubble cutouts covered the wall. To the right was a blank wall, which for the retreat functioned as a projection screen. An image of the event flyer with the title "Empty Tombs/Homes" and a foreclosure X lit up this wall. Along this same wall, breakfast was laid out for the participants as they arrived. Flipchart paper was posted on a movable plywood chalkboard. Opposite the focal wall was a bay of Gothic windows, and mid-morning light streamed in through the cloudy glass.

Metal folding chairs formed a large circle in the center of the room around a wooden table. This table was the day's altar. On it were symbols of the movement: an open Bible held together by duct tape; a wooden cross from St. Anthony of Padua–Most Precious Blood parish; a small black flag with the Spanish *RESPETO* in bright yellow letters; a song book from a partner organization called the Restaurant Opportunity Center in New York (ROC-NY); a black T-shirt with Harriet Tubman screen-printed in yellow with the United Workers' tagline, "Low-wage workers leading the wage to poverty's end"; a candle; a hacky sack; and two scarves woven by indigenous women in Guatemala. Liturgically the altar created a focal point. It also created a sense of the sacred with ordinary objects already infused with meaning for many of the participants. This type of altar helped concretize the struggle as sacred, suggesting it belonged not in a marginalized space but a place of honor.

With the space prepared, the participants began to filter in.[33] Some were members of the North East Housing Initiative, the Baltimore Housing Roundtable, or United Workers. Others were from the Catholic parishes that hosted the previous studies as well as other parishes across the city. There were Presbyterians and people from historically African American denominations. Some identifed with partner non-profit organizations like the Public Justice Center,[34] while others described themselves as social work students or as part of a volunteer corps program.

As people gathered, they mingled over the breakfast table, some catching up, others taking seats in the circle and waiting quietly for the study to begin. With a critical mass having arrived, the facilitation team called everyone to have a seat. They shared words of welcome and an overview of the day. The plan was to move through the first two parts of the Bible study, take a break, do the third part of the study, have lunch, and conclude the day with a focus specifically on the Housing Is a Human Right campaign. A participant was invited to share an opening prayer and light the candle on the altar. She acknowledged God's presence, asking God to fill the space and open the hearts and minds of those present to receive the Scripture as it was read.

Without words to introduce the text, I asked for volunteers to read Mark 16:1–8 aloud. The New Revised Standard Version translates the text in this way:

> When the sabbath was over, Mary Magdalene, and Mary the mother of James, and Salome bought spices, so that they might go and anoint him. And very early on the first day of the week, when the sun had risen, they went to the tomb. They had been saying to one another, "Who will roll away the stone for us from the entrance to the tomb?" When they looked up, they saw that the stone, which was very large, had already been rolled back. As they entered the tomb, they saw a young man, dressed in a white robe, sitting on the right side; and they were alarmed. But he said to them, "Do not be alarmed; you are looking for Jesus of Nazareth, who was cru-

33. All participant responses below are indicated by direct quotations, which I transcribed from the flipchart paper on which each small group reported their responses. While many participants would not hesitate to publicly identify with their responses, to protect the anonymity of particular individuals, and out of respect for the communal trust built by the group, I have kept all responses made during the retreat anonymous. I have removed potentially identifying details from the responses and have not associated responses with any particular individual.

34. The Public Justice Center is "a civil legal aid office that provides advice and representation to low-income clients, advocates before legislatures and government agencies, and collaborates with community and advocacy organizations." It "uses legal advocacy tools to pursue social justice, economic and race equity, and fundamental human rights for people who are struggling to provide for their basic needs." Public Justice Center, "About PJC," https://tinyurl.com/y3yy5bkx.

cified. He has been raised; he is not here. Look, there is the place they laid him. But go, tell his disciples and Peter that he is going ahead of you to Galilee; there you will see him, just as he told you." So they went out and fled from the tomb, for terror and amazement had seized them; and they said nothing to anyone, for they were afraid.

Three different people read the text aloud with a few moments of silence following each reading. With these initial readings this first movement in a Contextual Bible Study process sought to suss out "community consciousness," the collective realities, resources, and experiences of the people gathered.[35] It was also a moment to bring to light what interpretations might already be shaping how participants read the passage.

Accounts of the resurrection are foundational to the Christian tradition, so for participants raised in Christian communities, these passages were perhaps among some of the most familiar in the Bible. Participants had likely heard dozens of sermons on this text and its parallels in the other Gospels. While they may have been familiar with the resurrection story generally, what made the Markan account unnervingly unique was that the women did not share with other disciples what they had seen and heard. The Gospel (in what most scholars think is its original form) ends with terror and silence. By choosing this resurrection account over the others, the planning team hoped that it would create space to hear the text in new ways.

As the participants listened to the passage read aloud and began to settle in, I asked, "What words or phrases strike you in this text?" I also asked for a volunteer to record responses in the large group. A scribe took her place next to the movable chalkboard covered in flipchart paper adjacent to the circle. People began to call out words, which I repeated as each was shared. The scribe in turn wrote each response. The intention here was to affirm people's answers by writing them down to create a sense of transparency in which each participant could not only hear but also see each other's responses.

An awkward gap quickly emerged as the group waited for the scribe to record each response. In this instance it was caused not by a lack of facility from the scribe but from the responses coming in rapid succession. A participant asked if we could stop recording the responses. She felt the process was breaking up the flow of the discussion. While as a facilitator I had the option to slow down the group responses to allow the scribe more time to write, in the moment I chose to go with the

35. Gerald O. West, "Reading and Recovering Forgotten Biblical Texts in the Context of Gender Violence," paper presented at Contextual Bible Study Networking Workshop, Bogotá, Colombia, January 29, 2015.

energy of the group to keep the responses flowing. I thanked the scribe for her willingness, and she returned to her seat as the discussion continued. My intuition is that there was some initial nervousness about writing things down as the group started working together. While it was possible the participant who asked to stop the recording may have actually felt that the flow of the discussion was broken up, it was also very possible that there was some unspoken suspicion as to why the responses were being recorded and for what they might be used.[36] This adjustment helped build a sense of trust within the group and people's bodies began to shift from more closed to open positions. The discussion expanded further with the question "What is this text about?" To honor this moment with the group, the responses I remember are not included.

With this initial discussion in the large group around questions that opened the "community consciousness" of the participants, the interpretations and knowledge already present in the room, the study transitioned. The second movement worked to develop "critical consciousness" when the text was reread "slowly, carefully, and closely using the critical resources of biblical scholarship."[37] To help facilitate this slow, careful reading, the facilitation team broke up the participants into small groups. The facilitation was intentionally shared. The leader of each small group had already participated in a facilitation training and previous Bible study processes. Facilitating a small group became an opportunity for each leader to practice their skills and to continue to develop through the experience.

Each small group was organized around a member of the facilitation team who acted as a kind of guide for the group. From the large circle participants broke off into smaller circles, some using their chairs, some getting comfortable on the floor. The facilitation team provided each group with flipchart paper, markers, and an invitation to appoint a scribe to record the group's responses. While there was initial resistance in the large group to writing things down, the small groups began recording responses on the flipchart paper almost immediately.

Although there are several methods from biblical scholarship that could have been used to help develop critical consciousness, including thematic/semiotic and sociohistorical approaches,[38] the planning group

---

36. The indirectness of this participant's comment is an example of when the "hidden transcript" does not quite emerge from behind the "public transcript." The "public transcript" is "the open interaction between subordinates and those who dominate" and is "unlikely to tell the whole story about power relations," while the "hidden transcript" is a "discourse that takes place 'offstage,' beyond direct observation by powerholders." James C. Scott, *Domination and the Arts of Resistance: Hidden Transcripts* (New Haven: Yale University Press, 1990), 2, 4.

37. West, "Reading and Recovering."

38. Gerald O. West, *Contextual Bible Study* (Pietermaritzburg: Cluster, 1993), 27–41.

chose to focus on the literary dimensions of the text—its characters, their descriptions, and the ways in which they interact with each other. Issues of literacy aside,[39] anyone could identify literary elements like plot and characters. In some ways the use of literary methods was the most "democratic" of critical methods because they were accessible to everyone. In contrast, sociohistorical approaches required trained readers with knowledge outside the text itself. So, having moved into small groups to develop deeper critical consciousness of the text, each facilitator moved their small group through a series of questions.

The first question in small groups connected the focus text with its immediate literary context, Mark 15:42–47:

> When evening had come, and since it was the day of Preparation, that is, the day before the sabbath, Joseph of Arimathea, a respected member of the council, who was also himself waiting expectantly for the kingdom of God, went boldly to Pilate and asked for the body of Jesus. Then Pilate wondered if he were already dead; and summoning the centurion, he asked him whether he had been dead for some time. When he learned from the centurion that he was dead, he granted the body to Joseph. Then Joseph bought a linen cloth, and taking down the body, wrapped it in the linen cloth, and laid it in a tomb that had been hewn out of the rock. He then rolled a stone against the door of the tomb. Mary Magdalene and Mary the mother of Jesus saw where the body was laid.

Each small group was asked to read this passage, followed by Mark 16:1–4, and then to note similarities and differences between the way Joseph of Arimathea treated Jesus's body and the way the women intended to treat it. In terms of connections, both Joseph and the women were "preparing the body for burial." Both the women and Joseph showed "respect" for the Sabbath and "worked around it." Their actions were both "framed" by the Sabbath. While the groups did note some similarities, the discussions focused on the differences.

Joseph of Arimathea and the women used different means to access Jesus's body. Joseph worked "inside the system," while the women worked "outside" it. Joseph, through his position of relative privilege, had access to spaces the women did not. Joseph was able to go directly to Pilate to ask for the body. The women, by contrast, only knew where Jesus's body was buried because they watched the crucifixion and observed where Joseph of Arimathea laid the body in the tomb, both at a

---

39. Literacy levels can, depending on the group, present significant challenges in Bible studies. Some participants may feel ashamed to read out loud. Others may rely on the "oral tradition," having heard the text read aloud and reliant on their individual or communal memory of a text.

distance (Mark 15:40, 47). Only the women and Joseph knew the location of Jesus's body. The male disciples certainly did not. They had abandoned him at Gethsemane, and even Peter had denied him (Mark 14:50, 66–72).

There were also differences about what the characters did or intended to do with the body. Joseph wrapped it in a linen cloth. The women bought spices to anoint Jesus's body. While Joseph was able to carry out his treatment of the body, the women were not able to anoint Jesus's body because it was no longer in the tomb. There was disagreement among the small groups about how to understand Joseph's treatment of the body. One group described it as the "final injustice" against him because Joseph's actions seemed "rushed," while another group said that both the women and Joseph showed "care and respect" for Jesus's body.

One small group noted significant differences between the women and Joseph in terms of gender and social position. Each belonged to a different "social class" and "place in society." Joseph had wealth and power and was "part of the council," a person of political and social status within the Jewish community. Some participants treated Joseph of Arimathea with suspicion because of this location. Some questioned "who is he aligned with" since he was part of the power structure. And yet, what did it mean that he was "waiting expectantly for the kingdom of God" (Mark 15:43)? One group even went as far as to say Joseph's treatment of Jesus's body was a form of showing "care and compassion" for an "enemy." These comparisons and similarities demonstrated a detailed engagement with the biblical text among the small groups, which began to slow the reading in the development of critical consciousness.

The next question slowed the reading down further, moving from a verse-by-verse to a phrase-by-phrase analysis. The next question asked, "Reread Mark 16:6 aloud phrase by phrase. How does the young man describe Jesus to the women? What is the significance of these descriptions?" Mark 16:6 reads:

> But he [a young man wearing a white robe] said to them, "Do not be alarmed; you are looking for Jesus of Nazareth, who was crucified. He has been raised; he is not here. Look, there is the place they laid him."

These questions pushed participants toward an even closer reading of the text by noting the different ways in which the young man described Jesus. One group pointed out the irony that the young man "claims not to be Jesus but knows a lot about him." Another asked, "How does he know what he knows?"

The groups noted several ways in which Jesus was described. First,

Jesus was "of Nazareth." The description in terms of his "hometown" was of particular interest to one small group. Nazareth was a small village in the northern region of Galilee, an unsophisticated backwater in comparison to the more cosmopolitan Jerusalem. The group thought this detail "shows the humanity of Jesus" because he was associated with a particular place instead of an "otherworldly title." Another group noted Jesus was "crucified." Under the Roman Empire, crucifixion was an especially brutal form of capital punishment reserved for non-citizens who challenged the power of the state. This very public and particularly shameful way to die served as a warning against rebellion.[40] Another small group noted the detail that Jesus "has been raised."[41] A different small group identified Jesus as "not here." Jesus was defined by his absence. Some small groups concluded through these details that Jesus was a marginalized person, not someone powerful at the center of society.

The small groups found other kinds of significance in these descriptions. One noted that although the young man told them not to be alarmed, his words were "more alarming than soothing." The young man could have been anyone—a grave robber, an agent of the Jewish leaders or Roman authorities, or someone who wanted to steal the body.[42] In hearing the young man describe Jesus, the women had "turned-around expectations." They expected to find the stone still in front of the tomb. Instead they found it rolled away. The women expected to find Jesus's dead body. Instead they found it missing and saw

40. The crucifixion of Jesus was by no means a unique event in antiquity. To provide an example from the Jewish War (66–70 CE), during the siege of Jerusalem Roman soldiers captured Jews looking for food outside the walls while the city starved. The punishment for these rebels was torture and crucifixion. Josephus explains that the Roman general Titus's "main reason for not stopping the crucifixions was the hope that the spectacle might perhaps induce the Jews to surrender, for fear that continued resistance would involve them in a similar fate. The soldiers out of rage and hatred amused themselves by nailing their prisoners in different postures; and so great was their number, that space could not be found for the crosses nor crosses for the bodies." Josephus, The Jewish War 5.450–51 (Thackery, LCL). For a survey of crucifixion in Latin, Greek, Hebrew, and Aramaic texts within their respective historical contexts, see John Granger Cook, Crucifixion in the Mediterranean World (Tübingen: Mohr Siebeck, 2014).

41. A participant with some seminary training noted that the phrase "has been raised" occurs in a passive tense, that Jesus is not the one who acted but was acted upon. God is the implied subject that acts upon Jesus to raise him from the dead.

42. Another small group noted that the image of the "young man following Jesus" recurs in the broader literary context of Mark. When Jesus is betrayed and arrested in the garden of Gethsemane Mark recounts a "certain young man" following him (Mark 14:51). He wears nothing but a "linen cloth" (Mark 14:51). The men who arrest Jesus catch this young man, but he runs off naked, leaving the linen cloth behind. This mysterious "young man" in Gethsemane appears similar to the "young man" in the tomb. The reference to the "linen cloth" the young man wears may also echo the "linen cloth" with which Joseph of Arimathea wraps the body of Jesus in Mark 15:46.

the body of a living young man. This moment was a "radical reorientation."

The next and last question in the second movement went to the heart of this passage by continuing to slow down the reading, inviting the participants into another verse-by-verse analysis. This question asked, "Reread Mark 16:7–8 aloud. What is ironic about these verses? The earliest manuscripts of Mark conclude with 16:8. However, shorter and longer endings of Mark were added later. How is the original ending of Mark different from other Gospel accounts you have heard? Why are those differences significant?"

In Mark 16:7–8 the young man commanded,

> "Go, tell his disciples and Peter that he is going ahead of you to Galilee; there you will see him, just as he told you." So they went out and fled from the tomb, for terror and amazement had seized them; and they said nothing to anyone, for they were afraid.

Each of these two groups of questions implicitly used a different form of criticism. The first group focused on the irony in Mark 16:7–8 and continued to use a literary critical method. Every group noticed that the young man issued a series of commands to "go" and "tell" (Mark 16:7). The women followed the young man's command to "go." They fled the tomb seized by terror and amazement (Mark 16:8). But the women did not follow the young man's command to "tell." Instead they "said nothing to anyone" (Mark 16:8).

One group suggested the irony was that "they were given a direction, and nothing happens." Another group simply suggested that the "women don't tell anyone." The whole point of the resurrection was that it be proclaimed. But the women did the exact opposite of what was asked of them. If no one besides this handful of women knew about the resurrection, if they told no one, it was as if it never happened. The good news lived and died with them. There was a hiccup in the expected narrative. More than that, there was a hard stop, an ending with little hope of a new beginning.

The second group of questions, which introduced the manuscript tradition, added elements of textual criticism, or what is "behind" the text. Text criticism, as a particular form of historical criticism, added an element "outside" the text. While this kind of information might be accessible to the ordinary reader in the footnotes of an annotated study Bible, it was not available simply by reading the words on the page. This information pointed to the biblical text as a product of history; today's Bible resulted from the development of a textual tradition that evolved over centuries.

The scribes who copied Mark were perhaps so uncomfortable with its original ending that they added a second, and then a third, ending to bring it more closely into alignment with the other Gospels. One group noted that Mark 16:1–8 was the "one passage where people *don't* tell" (emphasis original).

These questions addressed the central tension in Mark's resurrection account: that the women witnessed the resurrection but told no one, and that the Gospel ended not with the proclamation of the good news but with terror and silence. The intent of the planning group was to invite the participants to be present in this place of tension, to sit with its emptiness, fear, and silence. The tendency, conditioned by the dominant Gospel narrative, is to move immediately to the good news, to the promise of new life. But Mark pointed to another side of the story, and as the earliest Gospel,[43] specifically to the trauma that marked how the Jesus communities began.

When each small group had worked through these questions in the second movement, the facilitation team brought them back together. Each group presented insights from their discussion. With this reporting back, the workshop turned to the third movement.

There was a break scheduled between the second and third movements. After the heavy lifting of detailed textual work, a break gave people time to decompress and process the discussion informally. Some continued discussions begun in the small groups, others caught up on organizational updates, and some just chatted about the weather. Whether directly about the biblical text or not, each of these discussions was an important part of the overall process.

The facilitation team then invited the group back together for the third movement of the Contextual Bible Study. After the slow, careful work developing "textual consciousness" through a variety of literary, text critical, and sociohistorical approaches, the third movement reconnected to "community consciousness" through an invitation to notice relationships between the biblical text in its ancient context and the "texts" of people's lives in today's context. This third movement did not draw parallels for their own sake but to address how the biblical text could facilitate transformation for the sake of the church and the world.

The facilitation team invited the group to return to their small groups

43. There is nearly full scholarly consensus that Mark was written just before, during, or just after the Jewish War around 70 CE. The Roman conquest of Judea and the razing of Jerusalem, including the temple, was the severe national trauma through which the Jesus communities had to process the stories of Jesus in order to retell them in the Gospels.

for this third part with instructions to consider choosing a different scribe and person to report back to the large group. The team continued to facilitate the discussion within the small groups. The first question in this final section laid the groundwork for the remainder of the workshop. It asked, "Are there connections between the empty tomb and empty houses in Baltimore? If so, what are they?" In their reports back, the small groups overwhelming perceived connections.

One group saw both the ancient tomb and present houses as sites of "condemnation." Jesus was condemned to death on a cross, while houses were condemned as no longer fit to live in. Both were sites of "abandonment." Jesus was abandoned by his disciples (except, of course, by the women), and houses were abandoned by what were most often absentee landlords. One group interpreted both as "manifestations of power." The manifestation of "good power" was Jesus's resurrection from the tomb. The "bad power" was property owners looking to take advantage of the speculative housing market, deliberately keeping houses vacant in hope of future profit. This group thought people who inherited or invested in vacants saw these properties as "dead," similar to the empty tomb in that they had "no potential." In contrast, multiple small groups thought both the tomb and the vacants were places of "potential" and "opportunity." One group specifically pointed to the empty tomb and empty houses as sites of "new beginnings" and "new possibilities." The tomb and the vacants were both sites of (potential) resurrection.

One group compared Joseph of Arimathea to the City of Baltimore's "Vacants to Values" program, noting similar power dynamics. This program had been highly criticized for contributing to gentrification and rising housing prices through facilitating sales of vacants to for-profit developers.[44] The group compared Joseph and the mayor as similarly powerful people and placed them in opposition to the women, who they thought represented the "community." This same group compared the determination of the women to anoint Jesus's body, despite what stood in their way (the stone at the entrance of the tomb) to people speaking

44. According to a report published by the Abell Foundation, a Maryland-based nonprofit with a focus on Baltimore, "Vacants to Value faces many challenges, including the accuracy of its data and outcomes, inadequate financing to propel more conversion of vacant properties, the thorny process of untangling property ownership, and the lengthy time it takes to renovate the city's long-deteriorated houses. . . . Its limited geographic scope means many of the city's most distressed communities are left out of this resource-intense effort. Most tellingly, despite the city's efforts, Baltimore's vacant building stock continued to grow in the program's first four years by more than 500 properties, with city housing inspectors citing 16,636 vacant buildings by the end of 2014." Joan Jacobson, "Vacants to Value: Baltimore's Bold Blight-Elimination Effort Is Making Modest Progress Despite Limited Renovation Funds and Questionable Accounting," *The Abell Report* 28, no. 5 (November 2015), 1–2, https://tinyurl.com/y45nz56c.

up today about their housing status to people in power. These people were themselves "powerful" when they demanded the need for permanently affordable housing despite the systems aligned against them. Both the women and people organizing for housing trusted that in spite of what seemed like impossible circumstances, they would speak and act out of what they perceived as necessity.

There was another thread concerning dissimilarities between the tomb and the vacants. One group pointed out that if the tomb had been "full," if it indeed held the dead body of Jesus, there would be "nothing to talk about." The disciples "want the tomb to be empty." Jesus's absence at the tomb was "positive." By comparison, an empty house could be "filled" with people and the things they needed to live. In contrast, there was no desire for the vacants to be empty. The group wanted the vacants "full."

Another group pointed to a different set of contrasts between life and death. They wrote the simple equation "home = life, losing one's home = death." The tomb simultaneously contained both life and death, the death of Jesus but also his new life, and the life of the young man found in his place. Perhaps Jesus was present through the women's encounter with the young man, just not in the way they expected.

One group compared the young man in the tomb to a "squatter," a person who lives in an abandoned house regardless of perceived illegalities. Like the young man, a squatter in an abandoned house was an "unexpected" presence, a "living person" where one anticipated only emptiness. While some people occupied abandoned homes simply as a way to survive, housing activists have also used "squatting" as an organizing tactic, quietly and sometimes overtly calling attention to the ability of people to fill empty homes themselves as a result of a desperate need for housing.[45] These comparisons demonstrated that after the deep textual work of the second part, the groups quickly began to make connections between the biblical text and their own realities through images of the tomb and the vacants.

The next question moved to addressing the housing crisis in Baltimore by shifting the small groups toward envisioning concrete practices. It asked, "What values, principles, and resources exist in the community to address the housing crisis?"

---

45. A more public, aggressive form of squatting is a "takeover," a tactic that requires a high level of organization and intentionally risks arrest as a form of civil disobedience. In the late 1980s and early 1990s, the National Union of the Homeless drew national attention to the housing crisis through simultaneous takeovers in twenty cities across the US on May 1, 1990. Filmmakers Pamela Yates and Peter Kinoy directed *Takeover: Heroes of the New American Depression*, a film that documents these takeovers.

The values and principles the groups listed fell largely into two categories, those from the wider US American culture and those from the particularities of the Christian tradition. One group pointed to the human rights principles of universality, equity, transparency, accountability, and participation that underpinned United Workers' concept of Fair Development described above. Another pointed to the principle of "people over profit," and the inherent "worth of people." Some principles were specific to housing, such as the need for "permanently affordable housing for all, not warehousing," as well as development programs that "do not result in gentrification." Interestingly, one group pointed to "home ownership." As noted above, this value had a complex history, but it was one that could be used to open conversations and meet people where they were. From a practical perspective, one group stated, "Existing homeowners value new neighbors in vacant houses."

Values and principles that could be rooted specifically in the Christian tradition but also have universal dimensions included compassion, stewardship, love, common humanity, and the question, "Who is my neighbor?" Another principle in this vein was the need for a community-based and "collective response." One group said the Bible "calls for action" and had "moral authority." Another group argued there is a "biblical basis" for connecting empty "dead" houses to living people.

Groups listed a variety of resources to address the housing crisis, including "churches with social justice groups that rehab houses" and specific nonprofits. One group stated that Baltimore's "housing stock" and "land" were not liabilities but assets. Surprisingly, another group included the mayor's office as a resource in contrast to negative comparisons between the mayor and Joseph of Arimathea in the previous responses.

This question about values, principles, and resources moved the groups toward the final question, which asked what concrete practices the groups would undertake to address the housing crisis in Baltimore: "What will we do collectively in response to this Bible study?"

There was a strong emphasis in the responses on education and "raising awareness," both internally among the participants and with the public. Relatedly, one group said there was a need to "challenge stereotypes." The stereotypical image of homelessness in US American culture was an African American man with mental health issues panhandling on a downtown city street. While these people without homes were one extreme and visible expression of the housing crisis in Baltimore and cities across the United States, poverty was far more pervasive and invisible in both cities and rural areas across the country. There was also a response about "connecting to realities that people are facing." While this group's idea suggested it might be a step removed from housing struggles, it did point to the need to center the lived experiences of people most directly impacted by those struggles when reading the biblical text.

Groups made specific suggestions about how to raise community consciousness. One group said there was a need to "replicate" the Bible study process with other groups and organizations. The planning team developed the workshop curriculum with exactly this sort of replicability in mind. Another group suggested the "expansion" of the Baltimore Housing Roundtable through invitations to particular organizations. A third group pointed out that in each of these practices, Christians were called to be "agents of resurrection" so that new life could be raised up in the Baltimore vacants despite the appearance of only emptiness and death.

With the textual work now brought forward into the world for the sake of transformation, one of the facilitators asked for a volunteer to lead a closing prayer. The workshop concluded with lunch. Like the break between the second and third movements of the workshop, lunch gave the participants time to process the content of their work together more informally.

This summary of the workshop has illustrated the three-part movement from community consciousness to critical consciousness and back to community consciousness, beginning and ending with the lived experience of the gathered community and reading the biblical text in an engaged way for the sake of social, political, and economic transformation in the present. It also served to build relationships with a broader set of individuals, churches, and organizations than had been engaged through previous Bible studies. This workshop represented a snapshot within the larger trajectory of the Housing Is a Human Right campaign, and this chapter will conclude by summarizing organizing efforts that followed this workshop.

WHAT HAPPENED NEXT

Just days after the Lenten retreat, Baltimore exploded in response to the death of Freddie Gray, a young African American man who died in police custody from a severely severed spine on April 19, 2015. Gray was from the Sandtown-Winchester neighborhood on the West Side, one of the very neighborhoods abandoned by the city and developers through systemic disinvestment. Fully one in every three houses in this neighborhood were vacant.[46]

During the uprising that unfolded in the days and weeks following Freddie Gray's death, Baltimore residents filled the streets in protest, drawing the national spotlight. Curfews were imposed, and the National Guard was deployed. The mayor infamously called the protestors "thugs." The national news media attempted to portray Baltimore as a city filled with outside agitators and stereotyped black residents as criminals. Playing images of a burning CVS store over and over again, the media missed the point about what kind of violence the city was facing and continues to face.[47] There was and is a difference between the structural, systematic violence Baltimoreans and people across the country experience every day, decade by decade, due to a lack of affordable housing and jobs that pay family-sustaining wages—and the momentary explosion of looting and violence in response to these conditions. The majority of the damage that took place during the uprising was to property, not people. The dominant narratives about the Baltimore uprising tended to criminalize people who are poor without analyzing the larger political and economic system that produced the conditions in which they live.

In the wake of Freddie Gray's death, the Baltimore Housing Roundtable and allies launched a "Fair Development Recovery Plan." This plan called on Baltimore City to issue a $200 million bond for strategic investment in the very communities affected by the overpoliced and impoverished conditions that led to the uprising. Partner organizations included the hotel, gaming, and food service workers' union UNITE HERE! Local 7 and CASA de Maryland, an organization promoting the rights of low-income immigrants.[48] The plan stated, "The outpouring of protests against police brutality in the wake of Freddie Gray's killing were the cries of a city demanding racial and economic justice for all. Applying Band-Aids is not enough; we must address the underlying structures of injustice that criminalize and exclude entire com-

46. Brentin Mock, "Baltimore Riots Flared in a Toxic Environment," https:// tinyurl.com/ y3uh53hu.

47. For insightful coverage of the social, political, and economic context of Baltimore in the wake of the 2015 uprising, see Sean Yoes, *Baltimore after Freddie Gray: Real Stories from One of America's Great Imperiled Cities* (Baltimore: Afro-American Newspapers, 2018).

48. CASA de Maryland is an organization "working to organize, advocate for, and expand opportunities for Latino and immigrant people in the state of Maryland. We do this by providing employment placement; workforce development and training; health education; citizenship and legal services; and financial, language, and literacy training to Latino and immigrant communities throughout the state." CASA de Maryland, "Who We Are," https://tinyurl.com/ yyyjfroz.

munities, impoverish our families, and evict us from our homes. . . . The people of Baltimore deserve a response to this crisis that empowers communities, reclaims democracy, and ensures the full range of human rights across the city."[49] This six-point plan outlined the needs to adopt a human rights charter applied to "all city policies and practices," including its police force, through the creation of permanently affordable housing and living-wage jobs; accountability and transparency in city government and private developer decision-making; equity in the city's budget and tax policies; and environmental justice through supporting green industries. While United Workers, the Baltimore Housing Roundtable, UNITE HERE! Local 7, and partner organizations across the city had been working on these issues for years, the uprising in response to Freddie Gray's death further highlighted the urgency of creating long-term solutions to the conditions that led to it.

That same summer United Workers undertook a massive canvassing effort on the East and West Sides of Baltimore to talk with residents about what changes they most wanted to see for themselves and their communities. Teams of volunteers went door to door with surveys and had hundreds of conversations on front porches and in living rooms about what social, economic, and political issues impacted them most. Concerns about a lack of quality education, affordable housing, living-wage jobs, and overpolicing came up over and over again. Hundreds of surveys were collated and condensed into a political platform named "Power of Our Potential." With local city council elections coming up in 2016, United Workers and UNITE HERE! Local 7 flipped the usual script on the electoral process. Typically, political candidates go to people asking for support for a platform they have developed. Instead, through this process, the community itself called on candidates to support their vision. They asked candidates to be willing to be held accountable if they signed on. In the runup to the 2016 primary elections, a number of candidates for city council and mayor did endorse the Power of Our Potential platform. Even Catherine Pugh, who would be elected mayor in the November general election, said in a candidate forum on affordable housing that she endorsed the Baltimore Housing Roundtable's vision for permanently affordable housing. (It would take two more years of organizing and public outcry, though, to hold Mayor Pugh accountable to her promise.) In a city with a long history of unaccountable public officials, communities across the city were working, through the democratic process, to shift that dynamic.

49. United Workers, "Building a Just Baltimore for All Communities: The Fair Development Recovery Plan," https://tinyurl.com/yxf43tly.

Just under a year and a half after the death of Freddie Gray, the Baltimore City Council and mayor approved $660 million in public financing toward the development of a new corporate campus for Under Armour, a high-end sports apparel and footwear company.[50] By the time this development deal became public, and despite ongoing protest during the summer of 2016, there was very little Baltimore residents could do to stop this "business as usual" effort. The negotiations had largely already happened behind closed doors with no input from the communities that would be impacted by this project.

In a city that already faced tremendous housing inequality, this development would build a corporate headquarters as a world unto itself, a city within a city catering largely to well-paid Under Armour employees. There would be no real effort to build affordable housing. The approved deal required that "10 percent of Port Covington's affordable housing units be built for people who make less than $26,000, but it contains what the critics call a 'loophole' that allows the developer to pay money into an inclusionary housing fund instead of building the units."[51] This inclusionary housing trust fund, created over a decade ago, had proven so ridden with its own loopholes that it has been largely ineffective, producing only "roughly 30 affordable units in eight years."[52] Despite these concerns, the city council passed the largest tax increment financing (TIF) package in the city's history, and one of the largest in the country, creating yet more public subsidies for private, corporate development. While the failures of the city's development model have been clear for decades, Port Covington became just one more example of the city's lack of commitment to permanently affordable housing. Through this experience it became increasingly clear Baltimoreans themselves would have to bring about the changes the city needed through holding public officials accountable and advancing their own solutions to the housing crisis.

At the same time Baltimore City officials were working behind closed doors on a colossal development deal that would largely ignore the very communities that needed affordable housing most, in January 2016 the Baltimore Housing Roundtable released a white paper articulating a "20/20 Vision" for developing permanently affordable housing. This vision called on Baltimore City to issue bonds worth $20 million annually for community-controlled, permanently affordable housing and $20 million

---

50. Luke Broadwater, "City Council Approves $660 Million Bond Deal for Port Covington Project," *The Baltimore Sun*, September 19, 2016, https://tinyurl.com/y2yjbp3c.

51. Broadwater, "City Council Approves."

52. Peter J. Sabonis, "Where Are Baltimore's Values in the Port Covington TIF?," *The Baltimore Sun*, April 11, 2016, https://tinyurl.com/y4jaez62.

annually to employ hundreds of city residents to deconstruct vacants and create green spaces in vacant lots.[53] This amount was a pittance in comparison to the $660 million allocated to subsidize the Under Armour corporation. Instead of continuing to subsidize private developers in the hopes that the profits would eventually "trickle down," the 20/20 Vision called for reenvisioning housing as a public good through the appropriation of public funds to support community-driven development in the neighborhoods that needed it most.

Part of this vision included the establishment of an affordable housing trust fund. In the summer of 2016, the same summer organizations across the city were attempting to make the Port Covington development more equitable and universal, United Workers and the Housing for All coalition undertook a city-wide effort to create this very trust fund. The goal was to put a question on the ballot for the general election in November 2016 to let voters themselves decide whether an affordable housing trust fund should be created for the city. In just over six weeks, a team of canvassers and volunteers collected over twenty thousand signatures from Baltimore City registered voters to get this question on the ballot. A major part of this effort was an initiative called Housing for All Sunday. During four weeks, over forty churches participated, opening their doors to volunteers who collected signatures from worshipers after services and during coffee hours. The Baltimore City Board of Elections certified the signatures, and the initiative appeared on the ballot that November as Question J. The question passed overwhelmingly with 83.4 percent of the vote.[54] With the establishment of this affordable housing trust fund, part of the infrastructure to implement 20/20 was put in place.

After the creation of the affordable housing trust fund in 2016 it would take nearly two more years of public pressure and organizing for officials to allocate money into the fund. Under the banners "United Not Blighted" and "Development without Displacement," efforts focused on the largely opaque Baltimore City budgeting process and a grassroots fundraising drive to demonstrate a public willingness of residents to invest in their own communities. Over five hundred people raised $40,000 toward a community land trust home in South West Baltimore. Meanwhile, elected officials had allocated no public money for the affordable housing trust fund. Reflecting on this contradiction, United Workers organizer Todd Cherkis wrote, "The Mayor's housing policy continues to be displacement either by bulldozer, gentrification, or

53. Baltimore Housing Roundtable, "Community Land Trust," 6.
54. The State Board of Elections, "Official 2016 Presidential General Election Results for Baltimore City," https://tinyurl.com/y34sangl.

negligence. Voters continue to act creating land trusts, raising money and this Spring acquiring properties to redevelop into permanent affordable housing. We know where this city's real leaders are."[55] At the same time as residents were calling for greater accountability from public officials from above, they were creating their own solutions from below.

When efforts to engage the Baltimore City Board of Estimates in the budgeting process were largely ignored, the campaign resorted to yet another ballot initiative to fund the trust. It was the second time they would rely on the democratic process when public officials proved largely unresponsive. This new ballot initiative would have "required the city to devote a nickel of every $100 in assessed city property value to the trust."[56] This second ballot initiative finally brought public officials to the negotiating table. "Faced with such a measure—and a history of voters generally approving such ballot questions—city officials negotiated with activists on a way to fund the trust."[57] In a major victory for the campaign, public officials agreed to allocate $20 million annually to the affordable housing trust fund. While city officials were quick to take credit, community leader and United Workers organizer Destiny Watford pointed out,

The only reason the campaigns have been successful so far is that they've been entirely rooted in the communities that are suffering the most from a shortage of safe, quality, and affordable housing in Baltimore. Residents have gotten tired of their neighborhoods meeting one of two fates . . . disinvestment and neglect, or redevelopment for the primary benefit of people who are wealthier than the current residents.[58]

While this victory was the culmination of years of organizing toward a vision of permanently affordable, community-owned, community-controlled housing in Baltimore, it was not the end of the story. There is still work to do in bringing this vision into reality. Existing community land trusts must be expanded and strengthened. New land trusts must be founded. Houses must be bought and rehabbed or in some cases demolished. Vacant lots must be turned into community gardens. There are home-ownership workshops to be developed and apprenticeship programs in construction to be implemented. There are door-to-door canvasses and leadership schools to be organized. The Housing Is a Human Right campaign is not over. In some ways it is just beginning.

55. United Workers, "Who Is Leading in Baltimore?" https://tinyurl.com/y576xyou.

56. Jean Marbella, "Baltimore Agrees to 'Historic' Funding of Affordable Housing," *The Baltimore Sun*, August 13, 2018, https://tinyurl.com/y3d9rrk6.

57. Marbella, "Baltimore Agrees to 'Historic' Funding."

58. Jared Brey, "Door-Knocking Scores a Victory for Affordable Housing in Baltimore," *Next City*, August, 15, 2018, https://tinyurl.com/y6xxqd7l.

At the same time that this work is about concrete change to the conditions in which people work and live, it is also about developing and uniting leaders with a shared vision for the kind of city people want Baltimore to be. It is about changing hearts and minds just as much as it has been about meeting people's basic needs. One of the gifts of the Lenten retreat was to deepen this vision through the language of faith, to be able to see both the empty tomb and the vacants as (potential) sites of resurrection.

4.

Facilitation and Methodology

Following two concrete examples of reading the Bible with the poor in chapters 2 and 3, this chapter takes a step back in order to identify the implicit aspects of both processes. Two levels of methodology need to be held in tension—what happens "around" a workshop and what happens "in" the workshop itself. The first section of this chapter addresses "theoretical" considerations that underpin the methodology, and the second looks at "practical" or "praxis"-based considerations specific to facilitation. As discussed in chapter 1, however, this methodology does not privilege intellectual theory over and against embodied practice. Rather it seeks a continuous and complementary relationship between theory and practice. The theory/practice of this methodology is rooted in ongoing, embedded processes for social change. The third section addresses challenges and pitfalls specific to the US American context, which are also considerations for facilitation.

METHOLOGICAL CONSIDERATIONS

As a Second Step

As described in chapter 1, reading the Bible with the poor is a second step. The first step is a relationship with and accountability to communities of organized struggle. Reading the Bible with the poor is a reflection on work already underway. The invitation to read the Bible with an organized group emerges out of relationships of solidarity that may have nothing to do with the Bible in particular or communities of faith generally. This invitation to read together emerges out of a need to reflect, and a need to develop theological and spiritual, as well as organizational, resources for ongoing work. This embeddedness is why chapters 2 and 3 include both the organizational history that was a starting place for reading the Bible with the poor and the processes that emerged out of it. Reading the Bible with the poor as a second step, as a process itself, is ideally embedded within much larger organizational processes underway before the Bible study workshop takes place and that will continue long after the particular moment of the workshop.

Text, "Text," and Con-Text

In light of the particular locations from which the Bible is read, a second methodological consideration is the intersection between texts and contexts. Reading the Bible with the poor always holds in tension at least two levels of text and context during the interpretive process. At its most basic level context is con-text—"con" meaning "with," or what is read "with" the text. The first level is that of the biblical text and its ancient contexts, both literary and sociohistorical. The second is the contemporary "texts" of people's lives, their personal stories, as well as the stories of the organizations in which they collectively participate. (A third level of text and context often held in tension with the ancient and the contemporary is reception history, received interpretations that create their own "text" and the historical contexts that inform them.)

The hermeneutical gap is bridged in connecting ancient stories of the Bible with the contemporary stories of people's lives. While grounding the biblical text in its historical context sometimes requires emphasizing its foreignness, there are also sometimes striking resonances between the biblical text's historical context and people's lives today. As demonstrated in chapters 2 and 3, there is sometimes a midrashic style of interweaving the ancient biblical text with contemporary participant responses. There can be a blurring of the lines between different types of "text," both ancient and contemporary. The process of reading can blur the lines of the mundane in the contemporary and the sacredness in the ancient, creating a sense of the sacred in the lives of everyday people through liturgical and reading practices as well as a centering of their lived experience.

In reading the Bible with the poor, the same rigor that biblical scholars use to engage the literary and sociohistorical contexts of the biblical text is applied to the contemporary context. In the same way that biblical scholars engage with materials such as archeological digs, parallel ancient texts, inscriptions, and works of art through the disciplines of archeology, classical literature, epigraphy, and art history—reading the Bible with the poor requires an equally thorough level of engagement with contemporary disciplines such as economics, political science, race and gender studies, and critical theory. I recognize that this is no easy task, and is typically not seen as the purview of biblical scholars. Biblical scholars tend to think it is their job or mandate to focus primarily on the biblical text in the ancient world, and that it is the work of other disciplines, such as ethics, to make connections to the contemporary context. Without a willingness to bridge the implications of historical work with the contemporary, biblical scholars risk becoming irrelevant to the lives of the everyday people with whom they have committed to building relationships. Engagement with the historical background *and* contemporary politics, economics, cultures, and ideologies that keep people marginalized and oppressed is work that is inherently interdisciplinary, and can blur the lines among "biblical scholar," "community organizer," and "faith leader."

The "Ordinary Reader"

A multiplicity of people playing different roles is needed in the processes of reading the Bible with the poor. These roles may include faith leaders, both lay and ordained, ordinary members of faith communities, trained community organizers, members of social movement organizations, seminary and university students at the masters and doctoral levels, professional biblical scholars teaching at academic institutions, PhDs increasingly in "alt-ac" or "real-ac" settings,[1] curious members of the general public, and so on. In my experience the types of people who find themselves in these Bible study workshops are, in the most endearing sense of the term, a motley crew.

Effective reading of the Bible with the poor includes at least three primary intersecting and overlapping constituencies: communities of organized struggle, the church, and biblical scholars or "trained readers." (The "church" here is broadly defined as the church universal, but it also may refer to specific congregations and individuals of faith.) I will address "trained readers" in the next section and broadly place everyday people and faith communities in the category of what Gerald W. West

1. In line with the trends of academia broadly, "alt-ac," the alternative academe, or "real-ac," the real academe, are increasingly the places from which PhDs work in contingent, adjunct, and non–tenure track positions. While many PhDs attempt to continue to work within academia, increasing numbers are moving outside it to find employment because of the sharp decline in tenure-track and tenured positions. Karen Kelsky, "Call It Real-Ac," *The Professor Is In*, December 30, 2018, https://tinyurl.com/y5da7gms.

defines as "ordinary readers." "The general usage [of the term 'ordinary reader'] includes all readers who read the Bible in an untrained or pre-critical way . . . the term 'ordinary' is similar to the terms 'the people' or 'the masses' as they are popularly used."[2] The words *untrained* and *pre-critical* are not meant to be judgmental in the sense that "trained" readers are somehow inherently superior to "untrained" ones. In fact, ordinary readers, from their social locations, often have insights that trained readers overlook. At the center of reading the Bible with the poor is an epistemological privileging of ordinary readers. Ordinary readers, because of their social locations, bring different kinds of knowledge, skills, experiences, and perspectives than those of trained readers.

Although it is important to recognize the differences among varying constituencies of ordinary readers, there is often significant overlap. For example, the organized poor are often also people of faith. Many of United Workers' leaders described in the previous chapters are active in churches and understand the Bible as a book that orders their lives. Reading the Bible with the poor recognizes that each overlapping sector brings unique experiences, perspectives, and knowledge vital for developing and implementing the reading process.

The "Trained Reader" and
the "Socially Engaged Biblical Scholar"

Drawing on the Contextual Bible Study (CBS) methodology, "at the heart of liberation hermeneutics is the relationship between the biblical scholar (or theologian) and the ordinary Christian 'reader' from a poor and marginalized community."[3] It is important to recognize in this methodology that certain types of knowledge "outside" the biblical text are not readily accessible to the ordinary reader; these include but are not limited to the sociohistorical contexts and the original languages in which the Bible was written. The socially engaged biblical scholar has an important role to play in leveraging this specialized knowledge into spaces where there might not typically be access to it. From my perspective, while a "trained reader" can be anyone with a "critical" approach to the Bible, regardless of one's ideological commitments, the "socially engaged biblical scholar" is a person specifically embedded within and accountable to communities of organized struggle that are working to

2. Gerald O. West, *Contextual Bible Study* (Pietermaritzburg, South Africa: Cluster, 1993), 9.
3. Gerald O. West, *The Academy of the Poor: Toward a Dialogical Reading of the Bible* (Pietermaritzburg, South Africa: Cluster, 2003), 18.

leverage the specialized knowledge of academia into dialogue with the specialized knowledges of communities of the organized poor.

Reading the Bible with the poor is not reliant upon "socially engaged biblical scholars" alone but simultaneously develops and empowers interpreters from the ranks of the poor. West explains that

> critical modes of reading the Bible enable ordinary "readers" to recognize the ideological nature of the biblical text (and their context) and to develop critical tools which will enable them to do their own critical analysis of the text (and context). The transfer of critical resources between their reading practice and the reality of their daily life is a central concern of socially engaged biblical scholars.[4]

At the same time, socially engaged biblical scholars are also developed and empowered through their relationships with ordinary readers. Biblical scholars are taught by and receive just as much, if not more, from ordinary readers as ordinary readers gain from biblical scholars.

In reading the Bible with the poor, socially engaged biblical scholars must recognize the relative power and social status that is attached to advanced degrees and specialized knowledge of the Bible. It is important that the biblical scholar in collaboration with the facilitation team recognize and decenter this status as much as possible. Decentering the role of the trained reader creates spaces for the voices of people who have been silenced and excluded their entire lives to be heard. While biblical scholars are used to lecturing, in reading the Bible with the poor their predominant function is to listen and to make available the knowledge of the academe when needed for the good of the group. To quote Arundhati Roy, "There's really no such thing as the 'voiceless.' There are only the deliberately silenced, or the preferably unheard."[5]

One of the primary ways the role of the socially engaged biblical scholar is decentered is through a collective process owned and controlled by the community of organized struggle itself.[6] An organized group takes the lead in constituting the space where the study will be facilitated rather than the socially engaged biblical scholar herself constituting that space. If the biblical scholar constitutes the group, the power of organization lies with the biblical scholar. The biblical scholar rather than the group has ownership over the process. But if the organized

---

4. West, *Academy of the Poor*, 48.

5. Arundhati Roy, "Peace and the New Corporate Liberation Theology: 2004 City of Sydney Peace Prize Lecture," *Center for Peace & Conflict Studies* Occasional Papers no. 04/2, 9, https://tinyurl.com/p443pue.

6. Gerald O. West, "Locating Contextual Bible Study within Biblical Liberation Hermeneutics and Intercultural Biblical Hermeneutics," *Theological Studies* 70, no. 1 (2014): 4–5.

group constitutes the process, the biblical scholar is accountable to the group and not vice versa. Another reason the organized group has ownership over the process is that the group itself determines its results.[7] What "comes out" of the study, the "product" of the collective process, is typically another collective process. The workshops in chapters 2 and 3 were integrated into larger organizing processes, and the development, implementation, and follow-up after the workshop constituted an organizing process in and of itself.

As with any role in a social movement organization, there is a need for the socially engaged biblical scholar to be critically self-reflective, to be self-aware of their motivations. Engaged biblical scholars must consider their own relative social locations, and their economic and cultural positioning in relationship to the organized group. Does the desire to "be of use" come from a place of "privilege" or "fragility"? In the words of an Aboriginal activist group, "If you have come here to help me, you are wasting your time. But if you have come because your liberation is bound up with mine, then let us work together." Does one's motivation come from a place of individual and collective survival being bound up in the survival of others, or from a distanced place of paternalism? It is important to acknowledge that no one's motivations are completely pure, that people are deeply conditioned by ideologies of oppression that inspire individualistic, self-serving motivations, while at the same time scholars can seek to be partially constituted by the struggle for individual and collective liberation.

While the paragraphs above have focused on socially engaged biblical scholars, each constituency that participates in reading the Bible with the organized poor—social movements, faith communities, and biblical scholars—represents different experiences, perspectives, and knowledge and are by no means homogenous within themselves. However, these differences also exist within the broader social and economic context that defines them and the need for liberation. As described in chapter 1, the bottom 80 percent of people in the US control only 7 percent of the nation's wealth.[8] This bottom 80 percent includes not just those directly affected by poverty or even low-wage workers who are part of poor people's organizations. This bottom 80 percent includes the vast majority of people who attend church and the majority of biblical scholars.

7. I am especially grateful for conversations with Sithembiso Zwane of the Ujamaa Centre for Biblical and Theological Community Development and Research for his insights on the relationship between communities of the organized poor and socially engaged biblical scholars.

8. Christopher Ingraham, "The Richest 1 Percent Now Owns More of the Country's Wealth Than at Any Time in the Past 50 Years," *The Washington Post*, December 6, 2017, https://tinyurl.com/yy6d9d6p.

Despite what can be real differences among these constituencies, they share the significant realities of a society defined in part by poverty and growing inequality. These conditions have the potential to form the basis for unity across the different constituencies involved in a process of reading the Bible with the poor. This kind of pedagogy risks developing biblical interpretations and theologies from the perspective of the poor in relationship to, and often distinct from, the prevailing interpretations and theologies of the status quo. Through decentering the role and relative power of the socially engaged biblical scholar, this methodology can inherently come in conflict with prevailing pedagogies, interpretations, and theologies.

Having considered some of the methodological issues in reading the Bible with the poor embedded within an organizing process, I now turn to some of the practical considerations of facilitation. While it may be tempting to dichotomize the above section as "theory" and the section below as "praxis"—as described in chapter 1—the movement in this methodology is toward cycles of action and reflection not distinct from, but inherently interconnected with, one another.

PRACTICAL CONSIDERATIONS FOR FACILITATION

It would be a book in itself to write about the art and science of facilitation, and there are many approachable resources that engage this topic. A starting point from the South African context is the Ujamaa Centre's "Doing Contextual Bible Study: A Resource Manual," which is available for free on its website.[9] Chapters 4 and 5 on the roles of the facilitator and participants in a Contextual Bible Study process are especially relevant. The principles articulated in the Ujamaa Centre's manual and the underlying structure of its workshops are the foundation upon which the workshops described in chapters 2 and 3 of this book are built. Another resource on facilitation I recommend from the US context is adrienne maree brown's *Emergent Strategy: Shaping Change, Changing Worlds*.[10] While not directly addressing a faith-based context, the principles of facilitation in this book are grounded explicitly in social movements and are particularly applicable to working at the intersections among communities of the organized poor, faith communities, and academia. With these initial resources, I will outline a few

9. Gerald O. West and the Ujamaa Centre Staff, "Doing Contextual Bible Study: A Resource Manual," https://tinyurl.com/yyyqvqe6 and https://tinyurl.com/y5oqp7qo.

10. See especially adrienne maree brown, "Tools for Emergent Strategy Facilitation" in *Emergent Strategy: Shaping Change, Changing Worlds* (Chico, CA: AK, 2017).

issues of facilitation that are especially relevant for reading-the-Bible-with-the-poor methodology once the invitation has been made by a community of the organized poor to a socially engaged biblical scholar.

Selection of Texts

A starting point in facilitation is choosing a biblical text. There are different approaches to selecting a text for reading within a community of organized struggle. Sometimes the choice of text is the result of discussion between the organized group and the socially engaged biblical scholar. Sometimes the biblical scholar may be asked to choose a text based on a theme the community has already elected to study. Or the opposite may also be the case—a group may already have a specific biblical text in mind. Some organized groups, especially those already affiliated with churches, may want to conform to the discipline of appointed readings such as the Roman Catholic or Revised Common Lectionaries. While connections to a specific theme such as a housing inequity or environmental justice may not be "obvious" in lectionary-based readings, the structure of the lectionary can work especially well when the workshop is organized around a liturgical season such as Advent or Lent. In sum, there are a variety of ways in which a biblical text might be selected in collaboration between an organized community and a socially engaged biblical scholar.

Curriculum Development

Once the biblical text has been selected, the development of the curriculum for the workshop can be organizing and leadership development in itself. The processes that created the curricula reflected in chapters 2 and 3 brought together a planning team representative of the organizations and constituencies who participated in the workshop. The planning included a series of meetings, first to discuss broadly and then to further refine the themes and content of the workshop. The planning also involved formulating the questions and developing the materials that would be used in each workshop. In light of the dialogical aspect of reading the Bible with the poor, discussion questions are a key component of the curriculum.

One approach to developing the discussion questions that form the backbone of a workshop is rooted in a "pure" form of Contextual Bible Study in which the facilitator asks "straightforward," one-sentence questions. For example, the classic opening question "What is this text about?" seeks to suss out the community consciousness in front of the text. Likewise, the question "What will we do in response to this study?" moves the group to the concluding step of connecting reflection and action.[11] Another approach is to develop more "chunky," longer questions that include information "outside" the biblical text, such as a brief introduction to the sociohistorical background of a particular passage. This type of question democratizes the process by creating less reliance on a socially engaged biblical scholar being part of the facilitation team to supply background information "outside" the text. While there are different approaches to developing discussion questions, they are the core of a dialogically based methodology like reading the Bible with the poor.

Alongside discussion questions, additional materials developed with an eye toward the replicability of the workshop curriculum might include handouts with the discussion questions or study guides with additional literary or sociohistorical information relevant to the biblical text.

Handouts versus Bibles

Related to curriculum development, a connected facilitation issue is the accessibility of the biblical text to every participant in the workshop. While often explicitly advertised as a Bible study, experience has taught me that a facilitator cannot assume participants will bring their own Bible to the workshop. Participants who do not belong to a faith community may not even own a Bible. To ensure that every participant has access to the text, curriculum development typically includes the need to create a handout with a copy of the selected passage(s) and study questions. The drawback of a handout is that the participants have no opportunity to "read around" the selected passage and are not exposed to the literary context in which it is embedded. In some ways this practice is no different than the use of excised printed passages in Sunday church bulletins, which are similarly devoid of literary context. While it has its disadvantages, a handout with the biblical text that ensures every participant has access to the written text regardless of whether they have brought their own Bible or not.

11. For an example of this "pure" form, see West et al., "Doing Contextual Bible Study."

Paraphrase and Translation

One of the advantages of participants bringing their own Bibles to a workshop is that typically at least a few different translations will be present. When reading the text aloud in large and small groups, the invitation to read multiple translations can encourage participants to notice the differences among them. This practice can sometimes provide insight into interpretation of the text when the differences among translations break open the meaning in the text.

Some written translations may sound more formal when read aloud because they do not reflect the contemporary vernacular in which people speak. Therefore, even with the use of a translation, there is sometimes a layer of "translating" in rendering the awkward English of a translation into a more approachable vernacular. This additional layer of "translation" can happen through a written paraphrase, such as the one used in chapter 2. Or, if the selected text includes dialogue and/or narrative, a dramatic reenactment in parts can also help the text come alive.

Another important issue with the use of translations is that not all are attentive, or consistently attentive, to the use of inclusive and expansive language. Many translations continue to use masculine instead of gender-neutral language, such as "mankind" instead of "humankind," and exclusively masculine pronouns for God. While I typically do not do my own translations for a workshop, I often substitute expansive language in translations when it is gender-specific. For example, if a translation uses "brothers" exclusively, I might change the language to the neutral "siblings" (even "sisters and brothers" can continue to reinforce a gender binary), or I might change the masculine "Son of Man" to the inclusive "Child of Humanity."

A final issue with the use of printed texts, including paraphrases and translations, is that there is often a diversity of reading abilities among the participants, ranging from people who are functionally illiterate to those who are highly trained. Many ordinary readers will "read" the text by hearing it read aloud because they struggle with the printed text. It is impossible to know the reading level of the participants before a workshop, and I therefore encourage inviting volunteers to read aloud instead of calling on people to read or "going around the circle." Those who feel confident in their abilities will respond to this invitation. Difficulty reading aloud can unintentionally become a source of public shame in a group setting. While the use of translations and paraphrases can add layers of complexity, attentiveness to the issues they present is an important part of the curriculum development process.

Democratic Organization of Space

Whenever possible, the workshop space should be organized in ways that allow for democratic and transparent participation. All participants should be able to see one another and be seated at the same level, ideally in a circle.

There is a truism in social movement circles that the revolution will be organized on flipchart paper. Also known as "butcher paper," a flipchart consists of large sheets of paper that can be posted on a wall with Post-It Note–type adhesive or masking tape. The use of a flipchart, in both large and small group settings, is an important part of the pedagogical process during a workshop.[12] The facilitation team makes a practice, either through the facilitator herself or the use of scribe, of writing down every response to the discussion questions on a flipchart placed at the center of the workshop space where it can be easily seen by everyone. Participants may be used to being ignored or deliberately silenced, so from an epistemological perspective it is critically important to affirm what people have to share. From a practical standpoint, recording responses also allows all participants to access the same information by hearing and seeing it.

Liturgical Elements

While both the biblical text and the "texts" of people's lives play a central role in the reading process, liturgical elements such as prayer and song are also critical. Reading can often be an intellectual exercise, while liturgy taps into the spiritual, physical, and emotional aspects that can aid in fuller interpretation of the text. Liturgy helps reading move down from the head into the body toward a more integrated, as opposed to strictly "rational," interpretation. It also works to create sacred space.

Liturgical elements in a workshop can include opening and closing prayers, the lighting and extinguishing of candles, songs at different junctures in the reading process, and visual symbols. It can be helpful to create an altar that serves as a focal point for participants. Include everyday objects relevant to the study, such as an open Bible, a T-shirt from the organization hosting the workshop, a vase of sunflowers like those described in chapter 2, or an image of the foreclosure X like the one described in chapter 3. The key is to use objects rich in meaning for the group gathered. Each of these elements helps bring liturgy into the workshop process.

12. West et al., "Doing Contextual Bible Study," 15–16.

Meals and Breaks

Breaks and meal times are an important part of the overall methodology because they provide both informal space for decompressing and alternative ways to continue the discussion. During a formal pause in the discussion, the methodological process continues as people often keep talking with one another informally about the content of the workshop. Things people are not willing to share formally will come out in side discussions during these times, and these informal conversations often raise up critical insights for the workshop as a whole. While these insights can contribute to the overall process, ideas shared offhandedly or confidentially should not be shared with the group, unless those who have shared these ideas give permission to repeat them in the large group.

While by no means exhaustive, this initial list of practical considerations in curriculum development and the workshop itself are a starting place for facilitators. There is also no replacement for the actual experience of facilitating and learning from the experience, which will provide its own insights and lessons. Before concluding this chapter, there is a handful of pitfalls and challenges in facilitation particular to the US American context that must be addressed.

PITFALLS AND CHALLENGES IN FACILITATION

The pitfalls and challenges for facilitation addressed in this section emerged out of experiences related either directly to those in chapters 2 and 3, or to similar organizing processes. They are particular to the cultural complexities of the US American context, although they could certainly be applicable to other cultural contexts.

Expectation of a "Banking Model" Bible Study

The format of many Bible studies in the US is centered on a pastor expounding on a passage, and participants only asking questions of clarification. There is no real discussion. Such Bible studies are a one-directional transfer of knowledge from the active position of authority to passive participants. This style is not so different from what Paulo Freire calls the "banking model" of education, in which students passively receive knowledge that is "deposited" in their "accounts" in a transaction from "teacher" to "student."[13] In the US, some people who

---

13. Paulo Freire, *Pedagogy of the Oppressed* (New York: Penguin, 1996), 52–67.

attend workshops using a methodology of reading the Bible with the poor expect to hear from an "expert" and are sometimes surprised and uncomfortable with the more egalitarian and democratic expectations of a collective, discussion-based process. Clear facilitation and setting group norms at the outset can help participants reframe their expectations.

Time and Culture

In many US American contexts—especially *white* US American contexts—there is a cultural expectation of a fairly limited one- to two-hour time frame for Bible study that follows a fairly strict schedule. The planning team for the Lenten retreat described in chapter 3 was challenged by the implicit structure of the Contextual Bible Study format that evolved in the South African context. It was not unusual for participants in a CBS format to spend a half day or an entire day in a workshop. There is, however, resonance between South African Contextual Bible Study practices and the way time can be experienced in US social movement organizations through what many colloquially call "movement time." Unlike what is often experienced as rigidly structured time in institutional settings such as schools, a product of white cultural norms, "movement time" can often be more flexible. I have found that people who are enculturated into movement spaces can have less rigid, less linear, and, frankly, less white experiences of time.

Another issue related to time is that shorter, highly structured sessions sometimes do not allow for building group cohesion and trust. By using a retreat format in chapter 3, the participants were able to engage with each other over several hours, which in turn created more space for trust to build. Taking time also allowed the participants to be more process-oriented and more aligned with a "traditional" CBS process from the South African context.

Another issue related to time in white US American culture is anti-intellectualism. White US culture has a deep current of pragmatism, what Willie Baptist would describe as an approach of "leap before you look," "shoot before you aim," and "act before you think."[14] The assumption is that there is more value in what a person does than what one thinks. Participating in a workshop process, taking time to think and study, is already, at least on some levels, inherently countercultural.

Cultural issues based on white US American understandings of time can present challenges in facilitating a process of reading the Bible with

14. Willie Baptist and Jan Rehmann, *Pedagogy of the Poor: Building the Movement to End Poverty* (New York: Teachers College, 2011), 141–42.

the poor, because this process inherently values slowing down and taking time to build trust and to learn from one another. Time for togetherness also bumps up against the US American value of individualism.

Individualism versus Movement Collectivity

An additional challenge to facilitation in US culture can be what is often an individualistic and spiritualized approach to Bible study. The collectivity at the heart of the process is a counterintuitive value. Despite the emphasis on the group, which is embedded in this methodology, participants can sometimes arrive and leave as individuals without a sense of commitment to a greater whole and without an embeddedness within an organization or social movement. Despite Bible study typically taking place in a group, participants often see the study primarily as having individual devotional purposes.

In the more individualistic cultural context, a devotional approach is largely focused on individual morals and on spirituality disconnected from the material realities of everyday life.[15] In addition to providing ample time to create a communal orientation, the Lenten retreat curriculum in chapter 3 deliberately included concrete and specific connections to the housing crisis in Baltimore and the ways in which movement organizations were seeking to address it. Although these connections might seem directed or even opportunistic, they reflect a cultural context in which a commitment to social change or exposure to social movement practices cannot be assumed.

Multiple Levels of Leadership

Finally, it is essential to develop multiple levels of leadership committed to collective processes for social change. For example, the group that planned the Lenten retreat in chapter 3 included a United Workers organizer, the priest at St. Anthony of Padua–Most Precious Blood parish, a lead volunteer from the Justice and Peace Committee, and me. Newer members of the facilitation team were encouraged to take on leadership roles by cofacilitating parts of the workshops that were organized. While

15. The distinction De La Torre makes between "metaphoric" and "material" readings is helpful here: "Reading the Bible to justify one's social location results in a spiritual or metaphoric reading of the biblical text rather than a material reading. A metaphoric reading is the process of interpreting the biblical text in such a way that its call for action becomes an intention or conviction of the heart rather than physical action to be undertaken. A material reading, on the other hand, attempts to introduce the reality of social struggles into the Bible." Miguel A. De La Torre, *Reading the Bible from the Margins* (Maryknoll, NY: Orbis, 2002), 46.

the planning process for each series became a form of leadership development in itself, there was also a need for a separate space to develop some of the "hard skills" of facilitation, such as managing group dynamics and reflective listening. Toward that end, the planning group organized a facilitator training to educate leaders and prepare for the Lenten retreat.

The purpose of this chapter was to illustrate the implicit theoretical and practical considerations of the methodology of reading the Bible with the poor, with an eye toward facilitation. While rooted in concrete experience and distilled into general observations, nothing in this chapter can substitute for taking the risk of practicing facilitation for oneself and reflecting on the experience with others. Like teaching, writing, or organizing, facilitation is a skill that develops over time through experiments, failures, and hard-fought lessons. There is no magic formula and certainly no perfect workshop curriculum. Skill in facilitation develops through grace, grit, and the gift of compassion from those with whom one works, and through the campaigns, organizations, and movements to which one is committed.

Epilogue: An Invitation

This book concludes with an invitation. It is an invitation, in the tradition of the African American spiritual, to "wade in the water." The movement toward liberation and life is like a river. There is a saying that "one never steps in the same water twice." The water is always moving, grounded in its source and flowing toward the ocean. This book reflects a step into the river at a particular bend, at a particular moment in time. Like the water that eddies and pools in a particular bend, there is much that has come before it and much that will come after it. Stepping into the river is an invitation to take the long view, to see the work of liberation, like the Bible itself, as the work not of one lifetime but of generations across the centuries. In the words of Leonardo Boff,

> We know how much our ways of speaking, our institutions, our legal system, our spiritual dreams, our religions and churches, our methods of socialization and of nourishing our imagination are replete with elements of power, authoritarianism, machismo, and anthropocentrism. We will need generations of Paulo Freire (the Brazilian educator who envisions education as the practice of freedom) and Robert Muller (the high UN official who conceived the content and method for a global and planetary education) to fashion ourselves a civilization for which education is a creative practice of participatory freedom and a shared life, an ongoing exercise of universal solidarity and synergy.[1]

This book is an invitation to be baptized in the waters of freedom, to claim one's right to be a tree of life in the practices of struggle and solidarity, and to claim the Bible reading with communities of the organized poor as one among many ways to go about this work.

---

1. Leonardo Boff, *Cry of the Earth, Cry of the Poor*, trans. Phillip Berryman (Maryknoll, NY: Orbis, 1997), 75.

In the tradition of the South African Kairos Document—which represents an ongoing process of theological reflection and action not only among church leaders, theologians, and biblical scholars but also with the people[2]—this book offers a method, a tool in the toolbox, toward further articulating people's theologies in the struggle for liberation. The continuous process of theological reflection and action among communities of the organized poor with the church and biblical scholars in workshops like the ones described in this book can contribute to the development of people's theologies. People's theologies in turn have the potential to serve as the basis for an authentic prophetic theology:

> The method that was used to produce the Kairos Document shows that theology is not the pre-serve of professional theologians, ministers, and priests. Ordinary Christians can participate in theological reflection and should be encouraged to do so. When this people's theology is proclaimed to others to challenge and inspire them, it takes on the character of a prophetic theology.[3]

Further development of this method in the US context has the potential to become a model for doing biblical interpretation that challenges academia and the church to engage in further dialogue with the organized poor and to be transformed by this dialogue. This model challenges the church and the academy to give up their positions as wise, strong "Selves" to come down to the position of the people and the "Other," where Christ himself chooses to be especially present.

Instead of in the halls of seminaries and universities, perhaps God chooses to be especially present in abandoned houses and polluted neighborhoods. But even more important, instead of in the halls of think tanks, corporate skyscrapers, and government offices, perhaps God chooses to be especially present with those who struggle for justice among the poor. We are each invited to be present where God has chosen to reveal God's Self, and there perhaps catch a glimpse of God's vision of a new creation among the struggles of the organized poor.

It is a faith statement to say poverty can and must be ended. It requires trust in a vision for humanity and earth that we are told every day, in myriad ways, is unrealistic, impractical, utopian, and naïve. How can human beings possibly live in right relationship with each other and the earth when so much stands in the way? To paraphrase organizer Charlene Sinclair, How can a person believe that after three days a person rose

---

2. Gary S. D. Leonard, "Challenge to the Church: The Kairos Document [Revised Second Edition]," in *The Kairos Documents*, 2010, 79n15, https://tinyurl.com/y2jjdjej.

3. Leonard, "Challenge to the Church."

from the dead, and yet not believe poverty, alongside white supremacy and patriarchy, can be ended? I believe in a God who does not want people to be poor, who wants people to live an abundant life of freedom. I believe in a God who calls us to rise, again and again, among the people.

Appendix: A Lenten Retreat Curriculum on Mark 16:1–8

BACKGROUND AND INTRODUCTION

The purpose of this retreat is to provide a resource by which to engage communities and individuals of faith. Its intention is to create spaces for biblical study and theological reflection through the lens of contemporary struggles for social justice—struggles that take place in a society increasingly experiencing the abandonment of the majority and unparalled abundance for the few. This study approaches the struggle for social justice through a human rights organizing model. In this model people of faith can be leaders regardless of whether they are laypersons or ordained clergypersons. It envisions that communities and individuals of faith are an integral part of the struggle for human rights and the movement to end poverty and injustice, because they, like all people in the United States, live in a society defined by a growing polarity between wealth and poverty.

This retreat is ecumenical in its orientation. The impetus for developing this study came from United Workers, in collaboration with St. Anthony of Padua–Most Precious Blood and St. Dominic Catholic parishes in Baltimore. United Workers is a human rights organization led by low-wage workers. Founded in Baltimore, United Workers is leading the struggle for Fair Development as well as for the human rights to housing, healthcare, and a healthy environment. Fair Development uses public resources to benefit the community instead of private profit and is guided by the human rights principles of universality, equity, participation, transparency, and accountability. United Workers is committed to developing and uniting leaders in the struggle for Fair

Development, a part of the larger movement to achieve human rights for all.

The themes of this study—the liturgical seasons of Lent and Easter and the current housing crisis—reflect the particularities and concerns of the communities for which this Bible study was first developed, but they are themes that are certainly applicable to other communities and contexts. The housing crisis in Baltimore, which is similar to the conditions experienced in many cities across the United States, was an issue of deep and immediate concern for the communities in which this study was developed. Despite the almost 20 percent housing vacancy rate in Baltimore City, there are two poor renters for every affordable and available unit in the city.

Human Rights

Human Rights Principles and the Fair Development Campaign

Most Baltimore neighborhoods are marked by vacant housing, foreclosures, unemployment, poorly performing schools, fire house and recreation center closings, and diminishing city services—an economic situation reflected in many cities across the United States today. In the past forty years, city leaders, in response to changes in the economy, continue to look to economic development and the privatization of public goods as solutions to these problems. Significant public resources have been and continue to be used to transform old industrial areas into tourist sites featuring restaurants, retail stores, and other forms of hospitality and entertainment. While this development produces some jobs, work in these sectors is often low-paying, is not afforded healthcare benefits, and lacks opportunities for upward mobility. It is also hostile to worker organizing.

These Failed Development policies primarily benefit private developers and real estate speculators, while most city residents and communities are still struggling to meet their needs. The Fair Development Campaign organizes for development and human rights that improve the well-being of all city residents and communities. The purpose of a multi-issue approach under the banner of Fair Development is to show how these issues are interconnected with others. For example, many foreclosures are due to bankruptcy related to healthcare costs. Fair Development must address all economic, social, cultural, and environmental aspects of people's lives in a coordinated way that connects different issue-based struggles and increases the ability of communities to meet their fundamental needs. As a human rights movement, the Fair Development Campaign seeks to build deep unity across all lines of division, including race, geography, gender, language, and religion.

To this end, Fair Development is guided by the following human rights principles:

- *Universality:* Development should benefit all and displace none.

- *Equity*: Development's benefits must be shared equitably and prioritize communities most in need.

- *Participation*: Development decisions involving public subsidies require public participation.

- *Transparency:* Development decisions must be open and transparent.

- *Accountability*: Publicly aided developers must implement development that fulfills these human rights principles or be held accountable.

United Workers' Human Rights Organizing Model

The purpose of United Workers' human rights organizing model is to build a movement to end poverty and injustice, led by the poor. At the center of this model is the work of developing and uniting leaders, especially from the ranks of the poor, as well as leaders from every sector of society who are committed to human rights values. Human rights values include dignity for all, respect for all, and the sanctity of life. Through leadership development and human rights education, leaders engage in "reflective action." Through this method of action and reflection, the power of the poor is built through organization, using campaigns as schools to develop and unite leaders. Organization and community are built through the Fair Development Campaign, projects of survival that meet people's basic needs, creating community through the arts, culture, and faith, and connecting with a network of organizations also committed to building the movement to end poverty and injustice.

History of Human Rights Organizing

One of the major historical inspirations for United Workers' struggle for human rights is the Rev. Dr. Martin Luther King Jr.'s Poor People's

Campaign. King was a Baptist minister whose speeches and writings were deeply influenced by the Bible. In the last years of his life, King's work represented a major shift from organizing for civil rights to human rights. In 1967 King realized that President Johnson's War on Poverty—as well as the passage of the Civil Rights Act (1964) and the Voting Rights Act (1965)—were not addressing the realities of exploitation and racism faced by the poor and dispossessed. In an April 1967 speech against the war in Vietnam, King spoke against the "tripartite evils" of militarism, racism, and poverty. Building on this stance, the organization of the Poor People's Campaign was announced in December 1967. By the launch of the campaign three thousand poor people, including blacks, whites, Latinx, and American Indians, would be mobilized in nine different caravans that would converge on Washington, DC. One of the major demands of the campaign would be the passage of an Economic Bill of Human Rights by Congress.

In March 1968, King was invited to Memphis to support a black sanitation workers' strike against the city and was assassinated there on April 4, 1968. In the wake of King's death, his lieutenants continued to organize the Poor People's Campaign. As "mule train" caravans from across the country arrived in Washington, DC, a shantytown named Resurrection City was built on the National Mall to serve as a base of operations. The high point of the campaign was the Solidarity Day Rally for Jobs, Peace, and Freedom on June 19, 1968, though Resurrection City was forced to close soon thereafter. One of the many lessons United Workers draws from the Poor People's Campaign is the need to develop and unite behind not just one leader but many. Another lesson is the importance of the unity of the poor and dispossessed across color lines, and all other lines that divide, in building the movement to end poverty and injustice.

Role of the Bible in Building the Movement to End Poverty

The US today is defined both by a growing polarity between wealth and poverty, and the pervasiveness of religion. Religion, especially the Judeo-Christian tradition, has historically played a significant role in shaping the values of people in the US through sacred texts, images, shared beliefs, and the organization of institutions. Christianity continues to shape the US context deeply as a "religion of the book." The Bible plays a foundational role in shaping the culture, beliefs, values, and ethics of people in the US, whether they specifically identify as Christian or not.

Like Christianity itself, the Bible has the potential to be both oppressive and liberating. It has been used to justify positions on both sides of every major social struggle in US history. Today it has the power to, and provides resources to, both sanctify and justify the status quo and articulate a vision for a more just society. United Workers believes that the power of faith can affirm the human rights values of dignity for all, respect for all, and the sanctity of life, and asserts that the Bible has a definitive role to play in the struggle for human rights in the United States.

METHODOLOGY

Through collective study, the stories of the Bible are brought into conversation with today's stories of the organized poor and the struggle to achieve human rights. The purpose of bridging this gap between the Bible's texts and contexts and our own is to explore ways in which these stories can speak to, and potentially intersect with, one another. This retreat, like any United Workers leadership development process, is one way in which to develop and unite leaders who are committed to changing the conditions of growing inequality and poverty that affect everyone. Deep and systematic study is one way leaders can unite to challenge this status quo.

The methodology of this Bible study takes both text and context seriously. The texts for this study are both the biblical texts themselves and the contemporary "texts" of the lives of people committed to the struggle for human rights. This method interprets biblical texts within their literary as well as historical contexts. It also interprets contemporary "texts" within their respective social, political, and economic contexts.

The methodology of this study is primarily dialogical. Through this discussion-based approach, the voices and experiences of the participants themselves are placed at the center of biblical and theological reflection.

Two major influences on this Bible study series are the methodology of "Reading the Bible with the Poor" developed by the Poverty Initiative at Union Theological Seminary, and the methodology of "Contextual Bible Study," developed by the Ujamaa Centre for Biblical and Theological Community Development and Research at University of KwaZulu-Natal.

Curriculum Components

There are several interconnected components to this curriculum for a workshop on Mark 16:1–8.

Notes for Facilitators

The "Notes for Facilitators" are a resource for implementing this retreat. It is strongly recommended that facilitators read through the "Introduction and Background" and "Notes for Facilitators" before organizing and/or implementing this Bible study.

An Introduction to the Gospel of Mark

A brief introduction to Mark is a resource for both facilitators and participants. It provides answers to some "introductory questions" about Mark as a whole, such as authorship, date of writing, structure, and themes. This information can be used to understand and interpret specific texts in Mark, as well as their literary and historical contexts.

Questions for Study

The "Questions for Study" are designed as a resource for the facilitator and/or as a handout to the participants. It includes the appointed biblical texts from Mark as well as questions in three parts. The three-part structure of the questions is adapted from the Ujamaa Centre's Contextual Bible Study methodology. The questions in part 1 focus on "community consciousness," drawing on the resources and experiences of the participants. The questions in part 2 focus on "textual" and "critical consciousness" and facilitate a close reading of the biblical text within its literary and historical context. Part 3 returns to "community consciousness" by connecting the biblical text with the experiences and struggles of the participants.

Study Guide

The "Study Guide" is a resource primarily for the preparation of the facilitators and can also be shared with participants at the retreat as a resource for further study. This study guide contains information that is primarily "external" to the biblical text in English translation. This study guide includes three major sections: "Context in Mark," "Key Words and Phrases," and "Making Connections." The "Context" section situates Mark 16:1–8 within its context within the overall literary structure of Mark. The "Key Words and Phrases" section highlights words and phrases that may be significant for interpreting the text as a whole. The section on "Making Connections" suggests contemporary resonances with themes that may emerge in interpreting the text.

NOTES FOR FACILITATORS

Who Are Facilitators?

Having multiple facilitators in this retreat allows for a variety of points of view and skill sets to be incorporated into the planning process, and provides potentially different styles of facilitating to be included during the retreat itself. With multiple facilitators the collective, dialogical methodology of this Bible study can thus be incorporated in its earliest planning stages as well as in its implementation. This retreat will consist of both large and small group discussion, including different facilitators leading the small group discussion in addition to those who lead the large group discussion, which can diversify the leadership of this retreat even further.

The facilitators need not be ordained clergypersons or otherwise consecrated leaders who are representatives of religious institutions. The facilitators also need not be "experts" in biblical studies. This guide provides all the resources needed to plan and implement a successful Bible study, and its contents were developed in collaboration with biblical scholars.

The Role of the Facilitators

The primary role of the facilitators in this Bible study is to enable the participants to engage in a collective process. Every participant is a potential leader who can be identified and developed in the movement to end poverty and injustice. Each participant has a role to play and experience to contribute. To enable this Bible study process to take place, facilitators need strong skills in managing group dynamics, encouraging contributions from every participant as they feel comfortable, and making transitions between parts of the session. Facilitators need to enable participants to engage with the questions for discussion as they are presented to the participants. It is also important that facilitators be able to create a space that is brave and sacred, especially as the issues discussed in this Bible study series may evoke deep emotions. Facilitators are not "experts" in the Bible. All the "answers" do not lie in the facilitators, although the facilitators should be able to provide basic information about the biblical text. It is okay to not have the answer for every question asked by the participants. When a facilitator does not know the answer to a question, rely on the resources of the group and/or plan to research the question further and to report back at a later session.

Preparation for a Bible Study Session

To ensure that the content of this retreat is well prepared, read through Mark 16:1–8 as well as the passages immediately before and after it several times. It is ideal to read the biblical text in several English translations (New Revised Standard, New American Standard, King James, The Message, etc.). The facilitators may note that English translations often vary widely from one to another, and these differences in translation can often indicate where translators are providing a unique interpretation of the original text. If possible, it is also recommended to read the biblical text in a second modern language, such as Spanish. (Recommended Spanish translations are the American Bible Society's *Santa Biblia* and *La Biblia Latinoamericano.*) Online resources such as Bible-Hub.com can be used to compare several modern translations as well as to look up words in their original Hebrew or Greek.

While studying the biblical text, also read the "Questions for Study" and "Study Guide" for the session. Reflect on how participants might respond to each question, keeping in mind that, especially for the questions in parts 1 and 3, there is no "correct" answer. Decide if there are particular questions within each part of the session that could be focused on more than others.

AN INTRODUCTION TO THE GOSPEL OF MARK

The historical context of both Jesus's ministry (ca. 30–33 CE) and the writing of Mark was the foreign occupation of Palestine by the Roman Empire. There is a general consensus among New Testament scholars that Mark was written just before, during, or just after 70 CE. Therefore, Mark was written about *forty* years after the events of Jesus's earthly ministry, or the span of at least one generation of Jesus followers.

A major historical event that deeply influenced the writing of Mark was the Jewish War (66–70 CE), which took place at about the same time that Mark was written. During this war, the Jewish people revolted against what was oppressive Roman rule. This conflict resulted in the complete devastation of the Jewish nation, the destruction of the Jerusalem temple, and the razing of Jerusalem itself in 70 CE. The references in the "Little Apocalypse" (Mark 13), in which Jesus tells his disciples "what will be the sign that all these things are about to be accomplished" (13:4), including the "desecrating sacrilege" and the appearance of false messiahs (13:2, 14–23), may be oblique allusions to events that took place during the Jewish War.

In order to write the story of Jesus, Mark was compelled to process this story through the Jewish War. The Jesus story had to be retold in response to the destruction of the Jerusalem temple, the place where God was present and Israel's identity as a nation was constructed. Therefore the "beginning" of Mark's Gospel is the beginning of a story that was supposed to be annihilated along with Jerusalem and its temple.

The traumatic events of the Jewish War, in which people starved to death during the siege of Jerusalem and thousands were crucified in front of the city walls for attempting to flee, are reflected in the style of Mark.[1] There are many "sharp edges" in the narrative. For example, moments in the nonstop pace of the story are in many cases connected by the word *immediately*. In the earliest manuscripts Mark ends in fear and silence (16:8). There is no proclamation of the resurrection by Jesus's disciples.

The author of Mark is anonymous but is traditionally attributed to John Mark (Acts 12:12; 15:37) as a summary of Peter's preaching (1 Pet 5:13). The "John Mark" in Acts has also been identified with the "Mark" in Paul's letters (Col 4:10; Phlm 24; 2 Tim 4:11). However, since Mark was a very common name in the first century CE, it cannot be determined with certainty if these people were the same Mark.

In terms of literary structure, Mark has three major sections, including

---

1. Josephus, *Jewish War with an English Translation by H. St. J. Thackeray* (Cambridge, MA: Harvard University Press, 1997), 5.446–51.

Jesus's ministry in Galilee (chaps. 1–8); on the way to Jerusalem (chaps. 8–10); and in Jerusalem (chaps. 11–16). Unlike Matthew and Luke, Mark does not begin with a birth narrative. Instead it begins abruptly with "the beginning of the good news of Jesus Christ" (1:1) and the appearance of John baptizing in the wilderness.

Mark is unique among the four canonical Gospels in that it has multiple endings. In a number of important manuscripts Mark ends at 16:8 with no indication that this ending is not original. As Mark began to circulate with Matthew, Luke, and John, scribes may have added up to three additional endings to make Mark more similar to these Gospels: a shorter ending with additional material, a longer ending (16:9–20), and an expanded longer ending (material after 16:14). These endings may have been attempts to "complete" Mark to follow the pattern of the other Gospels.

STUDY GUIDE FOR MARK 16:1–8

Context in Mark

This story concludes the passion narrative, which constitutes the last major section of Mark (chaps. 11–16). Jesus has already shared the Passover with his disciples (14:12–25), been betrayed by Judas and arrested at Gethsemane (14:43–50), condemned in the court of the high priest as deserving death for the blasphemy that he is the Messiah (14:55–65), and handed over to Pilate, the Roman procurator who governed Judea (15:1). Roman soldiers beat, stripped, and ridiculed Jesus before they crucified him with two robbers for the charge of being "King of the Jews" (15:16–27). After Jesus had died (15:37), Joseph of Arimathea, a man of wealth and position among the Jews, asked Pilate for the body of Jesus. Then buying a linen cloth, Joseph wrapped Jesus's body in it and laid him a tomb (15:42–46).

Key Words and Phrases

Bought spices, so that they might go and anoint him (16:1).

Among the disciples only Mary Magdalene and Mary the mother of James the younger and Joses, see where Jesus is placed in a tomb (15:47). All the disciples had deserted Jesus and fled when Jesus was arrested at Gethsemane (14:50). After following Jesus to the court of the high priest, even Peter denies that he knows Jesus (14:72). Only a group of women, none of the male disciples, witness Jesus's death at a distance (15:40–41) and then attempt to give Jesus some dignity in death by anointing his body.

As they entered the tomb, they saw a young man, dressed in a white robe (16:5).

When the women enter the tomb, they expect to find Jesus's dead body. But instead of a dead Jesus they see a living young man. Jesus's resurrection is encountered through his absence but also through the presence of an unexpected young man who inspires fear through his proclamation. Jesus is also described as wearing a white robe when he is transfigured (Mark 9:3).

You are looking for Jesus of Nazareth, who was crucified. He has been raised; he is not here (16:6).

This verse holds a contradiction. Jesus is described specifically as crucified. Under the Roman Empire, crucifixion was an especially brutal form of capital punishment reserved for non-citizens who dared to challenge the power of the state. This very public and particularly shameful way to die served as a warning to others against rebellion. But a man who should have been properly dead according to Roman law and order was no longer so. Instead he is described as raised and absent.

And they said nothing to anyone, for they were afraid (16:8).

On their way to the tomb Mary Magdalene, Mary, and Salome spoke among themselves, asking who would roll away the stone for them (Mark 16:3). By contrast, at the end of this story the women do not speak. They do not follow the young man's command to tell the disciples and Peter that Jesus has gone ahead of them to Galilee (Mark 16:7). They do not speak because fear has silenced them. The first reaction to Jesus being raised is not rejoicing but terror and amazement (Mark 16:8).

Making Connections

Where the women expected to encounter death, they encountered the living through both the young man's presence and his words proclaiming that Jesus had been raised. The resurrection can be encountered in unexpected, unlikely places and people. In the same way that Jesus was crucified ultimately by the power of Roman imperial law, today people's homes are "crucified" by a political and economic system whose laws condemn homes to foreclosure and abandonment. Just as Jesus was crucified yet resurrected, so too can empty houses become sites of resurrection.

STUDY QUESTIONS FOR MARK 16:1–8

[1] When the sabbath was over, Mary Magdalene, and Mary the mother of James, and Salome bought spices, so that they might go and anoint him. [2] And very early on the first day of the week, when the sun had risen, they went to the tomb. [3] They had been saying to one another, "Who will roll away the stone for us from the entrance to the tomb?" [4] When they looked up, they saw that the stone, which was very large, had already been rolled back. [5] As they entered the tomb, they saw a young man, dressed in a white robe, sitting on the right side; and they were alarmed.

[6] But he said to them, "Do not be alarmed; you are looking for Jesus of Nazareth, who was crucified. He has been raised; he is not here. Look, there is the place they laid him. [7] But go, tell his disciples and Peter that he is going ahead of you to Galilee; there you will see him, just as he told you."

[8] So they went out and fled from the tomb, for terror and amazement had seized them; and they said nothing to anyone, for they were afraid. (NRSV)

Part 1

1. Read Mark 16:1–8 aloud. What words or phrases strike you in this text?

2. Reread Mark 16:1–8 aloud. What is this text about?

Part 2

3. Read Mark 15:42–47 and reread Mark 16:1–4 aloud. What are the similarities and differences between Joseph's treatment of Jesus's body and the women's intentions to treat Jesus's body? What are the expectations of the women as they walk to Jesus's tomb? Are the women's expectations met? Why or why not?

[42] When evening had come, and since it was the day of Preparation, that is, the day before the sabbath, [43] Joseph of Arimathea, a respected member of the council, who was also himself waiting expectantly for the kingdom of God, went boldly to Pilate and asked for the body of Jesus. [44] Then Pilate wondered if he were already dead; and summoning the centurion, he asked him whether he had been dead for some time. [45] When he learned from the

centurion that he was dead, he granted the body to Joseph. [46] Then Joseph bought a linen cloth, and taking down the body, wrapped it in the linen cloth, and laid it in a tomb that had been hewn out of the rock. He then rolled a stone against the door of the tomb. [47] Mary Magdalene and Mary the mother of Joses saw where the body was laid. (NRSV)

4. Reread Mark 16:6 aloud phrase by phrase. How does the young man describe Jesus to the women? What is the significance of these descriptions?

5. Reread Mark 16:7–8 aloud. What is ironic about these verses? The earliest manuscripts of Mark conclude with 16:8. However, shorter and longer endings of Mark were added later. How is the original ending of Mark different from other Gospel accounts you have heard? Why are those differences significant?

Part 3

6. Are there connections between the empty tomb and empty houses in Baltimore? If so, what are they?

7. What values, principles, and resources exist in the community to address the housing crisis?

8. How are people of conscience called to respond to the housing crisis? Are there responses to the housing crisis that have not yet been considered? Do the responses that already exist address the root causes of the housing crisis? Are they effective?

9. What will we do collectively in response to this Bible study?

DRAFT RETREAT SCHEDULE

9:00–9:20   Welcome and introductions

Welcome to retreat space

Introduction of participants with name game

9:20–10:00   Questions for study, part 1

Large group discussion

10:00–10:45   Questions for study, part 2

Small group discussion with large group report back

10:45–11:00   Break

11:00–12:00   Questions for study, part 3

Large group discussion

12:00–1:00   Lunch

1:00–2:00   Housing Is a Human Right campaign workshop

Acknowledgments

The description in Hebrews of the "great cloud of witnesses" feels especially appropriate in acknowledging the people who contributed to this volume, of which there are too many to name individually but who are deeply threaded throughout this book.

This project would not have been possible without its grounding in United Workers, the churches with which United Workers partners, and the lived realities of Baltimore City. Without the initial invitation from United Workers to make trips to Baltimore and to build curriculum together, this project would not have been possible.

People who have worked especially on the Housing Is a Human Right campaign include Rachel Kutler, Amanda DeStefano, Adriana Foster, and Peter Sabonis. People who worked especially with Free Your Voice on the campaign to stop the incinerator include Destiny Watford, Charles Graham, Greg Sawtell, Rodette Jones, and Chloe Ahmann. I also can't forget Todd Cherkis, Iletha Joynes, Mike Coleman, and an innumerable number of canvassers, volunteers, and faith and community leaders who have worked tirelessly on these and other campaigns.

There are not enough thanks for Father Ty Hullinger, who opened the doors of parishes in North East Baltimore, and who took a risk among his parishioners with a bunch of ragtag, lefty organizers. His commitment to righteousness and justice is a model for us all. There were many parishioners from St. Anthony of Padua–Most Precious Blood and St. Dominic's parishes who supported this work directly and indirectly, including Ellen Marshall, Chris Lafferty, and Nancy Conrad.

There is a large network of scholars and practitioners across the globe committed to reading the Bible with and from the perspective of the poor. Thank you, Gerald West, for your generosity in writing a foreword to this volume, and for the invitation to be converted, over and over, to the perspectives of the organized poor. Thank you to the

Ujamaa Centre for Biblical and Theological Community Development and Research for allowing me to walk alongside you, and to Sithembiso Zwane and Simangaliso Kumalo for your conversations along the way. I'm also grateful to Paulo Ueti of the Centro de Estudos Bíblicos for your sharp mind and wit.

Organizers and scholars who have shaped this project here in the United States include Liz Theoharis, Shailly Barnes, and the Poverty Initiative, now Kairos Center for Religions, Rights, and Social Justice. Thank you, Willie Baptist, for bringing me into the work and shaping my vision for the future. A network of grassroots antipoverty organizations have shaped my development as an organizer, including Nijmie Dzurinko and Frank Sindaco with Put People First Pennsylvania, Sarah Weintraub from her time with the Vermont Workers Center, Desi Burnette with Movimiento de Inmigrantes Líderes en Pensilvania, Marian Kramer and General Baker (may he rest in power) with the Michigan Welfare Rights Union, and so many others, including Alix Webb, Phil Wider, Dan Jones, and Avery Book.

Important colleagues along the way have been Center and Library for the Bible and Social Justice, and scholars of the Poverty in the Biblical World section of the Society of Biblical Literature. Matthew Coomber and Richard Horsley have been important collaborators, and Noelle Damico of the National Economic and Social Rights Initiative an eternal coconspirator. Brigitte Kahl and Aliou Niang, alongside fellow students, shaped me at Union Theological Seminary in the City of New York, where faith and scholarship walk together to be a moral force in the world.

My church home is in the Evangelical Lutheran Church in America, which first claimed me at Emanuel Lutheran Church in Manchester, Connecticut, shaped me through Lutheran Campus Ministry at Boston University and the University Lutheran Church in Cambridge, Massachusetts, and sent me out with Young Adults in Global Mission to Pietermaritzburg, South Africa. In New York I was welcomed by Trinity Lutheran Church of Manhattan and Heidi Neumark, and the St. Lydia's dinner church. I now serve as the first person called to the faculty of United Lutheran Seminary in Philadelphia and Gettysburg after the consolidation of the predecessor schools, the Lutheran Theological Seminary at Gettysburg and the Lutheran Theological Seminary at Philadelphia. I will never forget the warm reception from colleagues here and look forward to continued work together.

Thank you, Fortress Press, including my editors, Mark Allen Powell and Scott Tunseth, for keeping this project on track to the end. I'm especially grateful to Neil Elliott for the initial invitation and for taking a chance on me at such an early stage in my career.

Without the love of my parents, Cindy and Randy Hall, none of this work would have been possible. My brother Curtis is the root of my passion for justice. He was the first to teach me about right relationship with the "Other" through being the sibling of a person with autism.

Muchas gracias, Luis Larín, *mi compañero en la lucha y parejo en la vida.* You helped to make a way when there was no way.

Selected Bibliography

Ahmann, Chloe. "Cumulative Effects: Reckoning Risks on Baltimore's Toxic Periphery." PhD diss., The George Washington University, 2018.

Alexander, Michelle. *The New Jim Crow: Mass Incarceration in the Age of Color-blindness: Revised Edition.* New York: New Press, 2012.

Anderson, Cheryl B. "Lessons on Healing from Naam (2 Kings 5:1–27): An African American Perspective." In *African Women, HIV/AIDS, and Faith Communities,* edited by Isabel Apawa Phiri, Beverley Haddad, and Madipoane Masenya, 23–44. Pietermaritzburg: Cluster, 2003.

———. "Reconsidering Theological Education in an Age of HIV and AIDS: Shifting Away from the Elite Towards the Marginalised." *Journal of Constructive Theology* 15, no. 2 (2009): 99–112.

———. "Transatlantic Reflections: Contesting the Margins and Transgressing Boundaries in the Age of AIDS." *Journal of Feminist Studies in Religion* 25, no. 2 (Fall 2009): 103–7.

Atwood, Margaret. *Second Words: Selected Critical Prose.* Boston: Beacon, 1984.

Aymer, Margaret P. *Confessing the Beatitudes: Ecumenical Edition.* 2011–2012 PW/*Horizons Bible Study.* Presbyterian Church (USA), 2011.

———. *First Pure, Then Peaceable: Frederick Douglass, Darkness and the Epistle of James.* London: T&T Clark, 2008.

———. *Repairers of the Breach: Five Bible Studies on Social Justice in New Orleans in the Wake of Hurricane Katrina.* Presbyterian Church (USA), 2007.

Baptist, Willie. *It's Not Enough to Be Angry.* New York: University of the Poor Press, 2015.

Baptist, Willie, and Noelle Damico. "Building the New Freedom Church of the Poor." *Cross Currents* 55, no. 3 (Fall 2005): 352–63.

Baptist, Willie, Noelle Damico, and Liz Theoharis. "Responses of the Poor to Empire, Then and Now." *Union Seminary Quarterly Review* 59, nos. 3–4 (2005): 162–71.

Baptist, Willie, and Jan Rehmann. *The Pedagogy of the Poor: Building the Movement to End Poverty*. New York: Teachers College Press, 2011.

Boff, Leonardo. *Cry of the Earth, Cry of the Poor*. Translated by Phillip Berryman. Maryknoll, NY: Orbis, 1997.

Bonilla-Silva, Eduardo. *Racism without Racists: Color-Blind Racism and the Persistence of Racial Inequality in the United States*. Lanham, MD: Rowman & Littlefield, 2003.

brown, adrienne maree. *Emergent Strategy: Shaping Change, Changing Worlds*. Chico, CA: AK, 2017.

Brueggemann, Walter. "Introduction: Reading the Bible Politically." In *An Eerdmans Reader in Contemporary Political Theology*. Edited by William T. Cavanaugh, Jeffrey W. Baily, and Craig Hovey. Grand Rapids: Eerdmans, 2012.

Cannon, Katie Geneva. *Katie's Canon: Womanism and the Soul of the Black Community*. New York: Continuum, 1995.

Cardenal, Ernesto. *The Gospel of Solentiname*. Translated by Donald D. Walsh. Maryknoll, NY: Orbis, 1976.

Cook, John Granger. *Crucifixion in the Mediterranean World*. Tübingen: Mohr Siebeck, 2014.

Damico, Noelle. "The Intellectual and Social Impact of an Engaged Scholar: Richard A. Horsley's Legacy." In *Bridges in New Testament Interpretation: Interdisciplinary Advances*, edited by Neil Elliott and Werner H. Kelber, 255–310. New York: Lexington, 2018.

Damico, Noelle, and Gerardo Reyes Chavez. "Determining What Is Best: The Campaign for Fair Food and the Nascent Assembly in Philippi." In *The People Beside Paul: The Philippian Assembly and History from Below*, edited by Joseph A. Marchal, 247–84. Atlanta: Society of Biblical Literature, 2015.

De La Torre, Miguel A. *Reading the Bible from the Margins*. Maryknoll, NY: Orbis, 2002.

De Ste. Croix, G. E. M. *The Class Struggle in the Ancient Greek World: From the Archaic Age to the Arab Conquests*. Ithaca, NY: Cornell University Press, 1981.

DiAngelo, Robin J. *White Fragility: Why It's So Hard for White People to Talk about Racism*. Boston: Beacon, 2018.

Dreher, Carlos A. *The Walk to Emmaus*. Translated by Paulo Ueti Barasioli. São Leopoldo: Centro de Estudos Bíblicos, 2004.

Du Bois, W. E. B. *Black Reconstruction in America*. New York: Free Press, 1935.

Dykstra, Laurel, and Ched Meyers. *Liberating Biblical Study: Scholarship, Art and Action in Honor of the Center and Library for the Bible and Social Justice*. Eugene, OR: Cascade, 2011.

Ekblad, Bob. *Reading the Bible with the Damned*. Louisville: Westminster John Knox, 2005.

Freire, Paulo. *Pedagogy of the Oppressed*. Translated by Myra Bergman Ramos. New York: Penguin, 1996.

Gafney, Wilda C. *Womanist Midrash: A Reintroduction to the Women of the Torah and the Throne*. Louisville: Westminster John Knox, 2017.

Goldberg, Abbie E. *The Sage Encyclopedia of LGBTQ Studies*. Thousand Oaks, CA: SAGE, 2016.

Goldsmith, William W., and Edward J. Blakely. *Separate Societies: Poverty and Inequality in U.S. Cities*. Philadelphia: Temple University Press, 1992.

Gutiérrez, Gustavo. *A Theology of Liberation: History, Politics, and Salvation*. Translated and edited by Caridad Inda and John Eagleson. Rev. ed. Maryknoll, NY: Orbis, 1988.

Hall, Crystal L. *From Cosmos to New Creation: A Call to Justice with Earth in Galatians*. Lanham, MD: Rowman & Littlefield, forthcoming.

Hall, Crystal L., and Luis Larín. "United Workers' Model of Organizing with Faith Communities: Unity across Lines of Division." Paper presented at the Annual Meeting of the Society of Biblical Literature, Baltimore, Maryland, November 22, 2013.

Hansen, Helena, and Julie Netherland. "Is the Prescription Opioid Epidemic a White Problem?" *American Journal of Public Health* 106, no. 12 (December 2016): 2127–29.

Harvey, David. *The Condition of Postmodernity: An Enquiry into the Origins of Cultural Change*. Cambridge: Blackwell, 1989.

Harvey, Jennifer. *Dear White Christians: For Those Still Longing for Racial Reconciliation*. Grand Rapids: Eerdmans, 2014.

Hendricks, Osayande Obrey. "Guerrilla Exegesis: 'Struggle' as a Scholarly Vocation: A Postmodern Approach to African-American Biblical Interpretation." *Semeia* 72 (1995): 73–90.

Himmelstein, David U. et al. "Medical Bankruptcy in the United States, 2007: Results of a National Study." *The American Journal of Medicine* 122, no. 8 (August 2009): 741–46.

Howard-Brook, Wes. *"Come Out, My People!": God's Call Out of Empire in the Bible and Beyond*. Maryknoll, NY: Orbris, 2010.

Ignatiev, Noel. *How the Irish Became White*. New York: Routledge, 1995.

INCITE!. *The Revolution Will Not Be Funded: Beyond the Non-Profit Industrial Complex*. Durham: Duke University Press, 2017.

Isasi-Díaz, Ada María. *En la lucha = In the Struggle: A Hispanic Women's Liberation Theology*. Minneapolis: Fortress, 1993.

Jones, Robert P. *The End of White Christian America.* New York: Simon and Schuster, 2016.

Josephus. Translated by Henry St. J. Thackeray et al. 10 vols. LCL. Cambridge: Harvard University Press, 1926–1965.

Julius, Marilyn Kindrick, and Luis Larín. "Baltimore Economic Reality Tour." Paper presented at the Annual Meeting of the Society of Biblical Literature, Baltimore, Maryland, November 22, 2013.

Junior, Nyasha. *An Introduction to Womanist Biblical Interpretation.* Louisville: Westminster John Knox, 2015.

Kahl, Brigitte. *Galatians Re-Imagined: Reading with the Eyes of the Vanquished.* Minneapolis: Fortress, 2011.

———. "Justification and Justice: Reading Paul with the Economically Vanquished," *Journal of Religion and Society* 10 (2014): 132–46.

King, Martin Luther, Jr. *A Testament of Hope: The Essential Writings of Martin Luther King, Jr.* Edited by James Melvin Washington. San Francisco: HarperSanFrancisco, 1991.

Leonard, Gary S. D., ed. "Challenge to the Church: The Kairos Document [Revised Second Edition]." In *The Kairos Documents.* Ujamaa Centre for Biblical and Theological Community Development and Research, 2010.

Liddell, Henry George, and Robert Scott. *A Greek-English Lexicon.* 9th ed. Oxford: Oxford University Press, 1940.

Lloyd, G. E. R. *Polarity and Analogy: Two Types of Argumentation in Early Greek Thought.* Cambridge: Cambridge University Press, 1966.

Lochhead, David. "The Liberation of the Bible." In *The Bible and Liberation: Political and Social Hermeneutics,* edited by Norman K. Gottwald and Richard A. Horsley, 128–41. Rev. ed. Maryknoll, NY: Orbis, 1993.

Longnecker, Bruce W. *Remember the Poor: Paul, Poverty and the Greco-Roman World.* Grand Rapids: Eerdmans, 2010.

Lopez, Davina C. *Apostle to the Conquered: Reimagining Paul's Mission.* Minneapolis: Fortress, 2008.

———. "Minding the Gaps: Reflections on the Fantasy of People's History in the Study of Christian Origins." In *Bridges in New Testament Interpretation: Interdisciplinary Advances,* edited by Neil Elliott and Werner H. Kelber, 255–310. New York: Lexington, 2018.

Lorde, Audre. *Sister Outsider: Essays and Speeches.* Berkley: Crossing, 1984.

Meggit, Justin J. *Paul, Poverty and Survival.* Edinburgh: T&T Clark, 1998.

Nadar, Sarojini. "Beyond the 'Ordinary Reader' and the 'Invisible Intellectual': Pushing the Boundaries of Contextual Bible Study Discourses." In *The Future of the Biblical Past: Envisioning Biblical Studies on a Global Key,* edited by Roland Boer and Fernando F. Segovia, 13–28. Atlanta: Society of Biblical Literature, 2012.

Okun, Tema. *The Emperor Has No Clothes: Teaching about Race and Racism to People Who Don't Want to Know.* Charlotte, NC: Information Age, 2010.

Osborne, Robin. Introduction to *Poverty in the Roman World*, edited by Margaret Atkins and Robin Osborne, 1–20. New York: Cambridge University Press, 2006.

Pietila, Antero. *Not in My Neighborhood: How Bigotry Shaped a Great American City.* Chicago: Ivan R. Dee, 2010.

Pithouse, Richard. "Struggle Is a School: The Rise of the Shackdwellers' Movement in Durban, South Africa." *Monthly Review* 57, no. 9 (February 1, 2006): 30–51.

Powery, Emerson B., and Rodney S. Sadler Jr. *The Genesis of Liberation: Biblical Interpretation in the Antebellum Narratives of the Enslaved.* Louisville: Westminster John Knox, 2016.

Rathbone, Dominic. "Poverty and Population in Roman Egypt." In *Poverty in the Roman World*, edited by Margaret Atkins and Robin Osborne, 100–114. New York: Cambridge University Press, 2006.

Rehmann, Jan. *Theories of Ideology: The Powers of Alienation and Subjection.* Boston: Brill, 2013.

Riches, John. *What Is Contextual Bible Study?: A Practical Guide with Group Studies for Advent and Lent.* London: Society for Promoting Christian Knowledge, 2010.

Rieger, Joerg, and Kwok Pui-lan. *Occupy Religion: Theology of the Multitude.* Lanham, MD: Rowman & Littlefield, 2012.

Roy, Arundhati. "Peace and the New Corporate Liberation Theology: 2004 City of Sydney Peace Prize Lecture." Center for Peace and Conflict Studies Occasional Papers no. 04/2.

Schüssler Fiorenza, Elisabeth. *In Memory of Her: A Feminist Theological Reconstruction of Christian Origins.* New York: Crossroad, 1983.

Scott, James C. *Domination and the Arts of Resistance: Hidden Transcripts.* New Haven: Yale University Press, 1990.

———. *Weapons of the Weak: Everyday Forms of Peasant Resistance.* New Haven: Yale University Press, 1985.

Segovia, Fernando F. "Mujerista Theology: Biblical Interpretation and Political Theology." *Feminist Theology* 20, no. 1 (September 2011): 21–27.

Shannon, S. K. S., C. Uggen, J. Schnittker, et al. "The Growth, Scope, and Spatial Distribution of People with Felony Records in the United States, 1948–2010." *Demography* 54 (2017): 1795–1818.

Shoffren, Marc. "Educational Approaches to Naboth's Vineyard (1 Kings 21)." *The Journal of Progressive Judaism* 13 (November 1999): 7–18.

Sonnie, Amy, and James Tracy. *Hillbilly Nationalists, Urban Race Rebels, and Black Power: Community Organizing in Radical Times.* Brooklyn: Melville House, 2011.

Stanton, Elizabeth Cady. *The Woman's Bible.* New York: Arno, 1972.

Taylor, Marion Ann, and Agnes Choi, eds. *Handbook of Women Biblical Interpreters: A Historical and Biographical Guide.* Grand Rapids: Baker Academic, 2012.

Theoharis, Liz. *Always with Us? What Jesus Really Said about the Poor.* Grand Rapids: Eerdmans, 2017.

Theoharis, Liz, and Willie Baptist. "Reading the Bible with the Poor: Building a Social Movement Led by the Poor, as a United Social Force." In *Reading the Bible in Age of Crisis: Political Exegesis for a New Day*, edited by Bruce Worthington, 21–52. Minneapolis: Fortress, 2015.

Trible, Phyllis. *God and the Rhetoric of Sexuality.* Philadelphia: Fortress, 1978.

Wachowski, Lana, and Lilly Wachowski. *The Matrix.* Los Angeles: Warner Bros., 1999.

Wallis, Jim. *Racism, White Privilege and the Bridge to a New America.* Grand Rapids: Brazos, 2016.

West, Gerald O. *The Academy of the Poor: Towards a Dialogical Reading of the Bible.* Sheffield: Sheffield Academic, 1999.

———. *Biblical Hermeneutics of Liberation: Modes of Reading the Bible in the South African Context.* Maryknoll, NY: Orbis, 1995.

———. *Contextual Bible Study.* Pietermaritzburg: Cluster, 1993.

———. "Locating Contextual Bible Study within Biblical Liberation Hermeneutics and Intercultural Biblical Hermeneutics." *Theological Studies* 70, no. 1 (2014).

———. "Reading and Recovering Forgotten Biblical Texts in the Context of Gender Violence." Paper presented at Contextual Bible Study Networking Workshop, Bogotá, Colombia, January 29, 2015.

———, ed. *Reading Other-Wise: Socially Engaged Biblical Scholars Reading with Their Local Communities.* Boston: Brill, 2007.

West, Gerald O., and Phumzile Zondi-Mabizela. "The Bible Story That Became a Campaign: The Tamar Campaign in South Africa (and Beyond)." *Ministerial Formation* 103 (July 2004): 4–12.

Wright, M. R. *Cosmology in Antiquity.* New York: Routledge, 1995.

Wylie-Kellermann, Bill. *Where the Water Goes Around: Beloved Detroit.* Eugene, OR: Cascade, 2017.

Yoes, Sean. *Baltimore after Freddie Gray: Real Stories from One of America's Great Imperiled Cities*. Baltimore: Afro-American Newspapers, 2018.

Subject Index

Baltimore, xvii–xviii, xxii, xxiv, 30-36, 38-42, 45, 50-53, 55, 57-68, 70, 78-87, 102, 109-10, 121, 123; Curtis Bay, 33-35, 37-43, 41-43, 49-51, 54-55
Baltimore Housing Roundtable, 59–60, 62–67, 70, 81–85
biblical scholars, xix–xxxii, 13, 20, 24, 27–28, 46, 90–91, 93–94, 106, 115

capitalism, 5-6, 9-12, 15, 18, 22, 26, 30; deindustrialization, 32, 58-59; neoliberalism, 32
Centro de Estudos Bíblicos, xx–xxi, 124
church(es), xvii–xxii, 4, 19–21, 25, 28, 42, 52, 66-67, 77, 80–81, 85, 91-92, 94, 97, 105-6, 123-24
community land trust, 64–66, 85-86
Contextual Bible Study, xvii, xix–xxi, 19, 20, 24, 44, 54, 71–72, 77, 92, 95–96, 101, 113–14
criticism, biblical, 28, 76; historical, 28, 76; literary, 29

curriculum, 29, 41–42, 66–67, 69, 81, 102–3, 114, 123; development, 29, 41, 96–98, 100

epistemology, 1, 99; epistemological privilege, 29–30, 92

facilitation, 72, 95–100; pitfalls, 100–103
foreclosure, 68–69, 99, 110, 120

hidden and public transcripts, xvii, 72
Housing Our Neighbors, 59, 62–63
human rights, xix, xxiv, 17, 35–37, 39, 54–55, 61–62, 67, 70, 80, 83, 109–13

ideology, 4–9, 12, 14, 16, 26; of oppression, 6–9, 12, 16
individualism, 9, 65, 102
inequality, xix, xxiii, 10–11, 14, 32, 61–62, 95 ; housing, 84; income, 10; racial, 7; wealth, 10–11
internalized oppression, 15–16
intersectionality, 15

Kairos Center for Religions, Rights
    and Social Justice, xxi, 10, 13,
    66–67, 124

liberation, xix, xxi–xxiii, 1, 17–24,
    27–30, 92, 94, 105–6;
    hermeneutics, 20, 29, 92; theol-
    ogy, xxi, 19, 28
liturgy, 67, 69, 90, 96, 99, 110

organized poor, xviii–xxi,
    xxiii–xxiv, 1, 18–20, 24–27,
    29–30, 51, 92–96, 105–6, 113,
    123

patriarchy, 7–9
poverty, xviii–xvix, xxi–xxii, 2, 4,
    11–15, 17, 21, 25, 31–33, 35,
    55, 60–61, 69, 80, 94–95,
    106–7, 109, 111–13, 115; theo-
    ries of impoverishment, xvi, 13,
    31
pragmatism, 4, 101
praxis, xxii, 3, 89, 95

reader: ordinary, 27, 29, 44, 76,
    91–92; trained, xxii, 24–25, 30,
    92–95

socially engaged biblical scholar,
    xvii, 2, 24, 27, 92–97

text, biblical, xx, 28, 41, 43, 45–49,
    51, 57, 74, 76–77, 79, 81,
    90–93, 96–97, 99, 102, 113–16;
    context, 48–49, 51, 77; selec-
    tion, 41, 96; translation, 98

Ujamaa Centre for Biblical and
    Theological Community
    Development and Research,
    xix–xxi, 25, 94–95, 113, 124
United Workers, xxiv, 30, 35–38,
    41–42, 45, 52, 58, 61–63.
    65–67, 69–70, 80, 83, 85–86,
    92, 102, 109, 111–13, 123; Fair
    Development, 35–38, 52, 62,
    67, 80, 82, 109–11; Free Your
    Voice, xxiv, 37–42, 51–55, 123

white supremacy, 1, 5–9, 10–11,
    15–16, 18, 22, 26, 30, 107;
    racism, 7, 9, 15–16, 19, 31–32,
    58–59, 112

Scripture Index